THE GAME OF BOWLS

Also by David Bryant

BRYANT ON BOWLS
BOWL WITH BRYANT

THE GAME OF BOWLS
DAVID BRYANT
& DAVID RHYS JONES

PARTRIDGE PRESS

LONDON · NEW YORK · TORONTO · SYDNEY · AUCKLAND

TRANSWORLD
PUBLISHERS LTD
61-63 Uxbridge Road, London
W5 5SA

TRANSWORLD
PUBLISHERS (AUSTRALIA)
PTY LTD
15-23 Helles Avenue,
Moorebank, NSW 2170

TRANSWORLD
PUBLISHERS (NZ) LTD
Cnr Moselle and Waipareira
Aves,
Henderson, Auckland

Published 1990 by Partridge
Press
a division of Transworld
Publishers Ltd
Copyright © David Bryant
and David Rhys Jones 1990

British Library Cataloguing
in Publication Data
Bryant, David *1931 –*
  The game of bowls.
  1. Ball games. Bowls
  I. Title   II. Rhys Jones,
  David
  796.31

  ISBN 1-85225-101-8

Printed in Great Britain
by Butler and Tanner Ltd, Frome

FOR OUR FAMILIES
Our fathers, Reg Bryant and Charles Jones, for their good example; Our wives, Ruth Bryant and Jill Rhys Jones, for their support; Our children, Jacqui and Carole Bryant and Corin and Cerys Rhys Jones for their patience.

Acknowledgements
Thank you to Duncan Cubitt of Bowls International and Maurice Sims of Clevedon for the majority of the photographs.

CONTENTS

INTRODUCTION

Bowls is a family game. The vast majority of top players have come into the game because their fathers played — and perhaps their mothers, too. Thinking of the current England team, Tony Allcock's mother, Joan, was an England international and Brett Morley's dad, Stan, played for England.

The famous Ward family from Norfolk can boast two brothers, Chris and David, and a sister, Jayne Roylance, who are all internationals. Chris and David won the bronze medal at Balgreen in the 1986 Commonwealth Games, and Jayne was part of England's team that won the world title in 1988. They were introduced to bowls by their father, George.

We, the two Davids, were introduced to bowls by our parents, Reg Bryant and Charles Jones, and owe a great deal to their influence. Reg was an English indoor international, while Charles was a Carmarthenshire county skip for many years.

We used to sit for hours, watching bowls, before we ever rolled a wood, one of us in Clevedon in the 1930s, and the other in Llanelli in the 1940s — and early holidays were also spent at tournaments, either by the seaside or at inland spas like Llandrindod Wells.

It's a marvellous thing that bowls has developed the way it has — making it much more normal for youngsters to be introduced to the game. In our day, it was an exception to meet a bowler who was under forty, let alone twenty! Now teenagers are two a penny — and very good they often are too.

So, the sight — a common one at our own club, Clevedon — of three generations of the same family

enjoying a roll-up together, is probably repeated in many clubs all over England, and perhaps all over the world. At Clevedon, Doug Sweet is proud to partner his son, Bob, and grandson, Derek – and a formidable triple they make.

A Bristol family triple, Paul Horsted and his father, John and grandad, Bob, won the Weston St Andrews open triples recently, interrupting their caravan holiday in Cornwall to play the final day, and returning to the holiday camp to celebrate with a lap of honour, cup held high, at midnight.

Reading the biographies of the top stars, it seems that most of them started playing bowls in their early teens, if not before. Noel Burrows, a great crown green bowler who has adapted successfully to the level green game, says he started at the age of four.

And, at the other end of the scale, the Aberystwyth Open singles was won in 1988 by Ted Hamer, at the ripe old age of eighty-one, while Lilian Nicholas, a grand stalwart of Welsh women's bowls,

The Sweet family – from the authors' club in Clevedon – provide evidence that bowls is a game for all the family.
(l-r Bob, Derek and Doug)
(Bob Bowen)

competed in the British indoor championships when she was eighty.

No wonder bowls is such a popular family game, and is likely to become even more so as the game opens up to mixed play. No other active outdoor sport allows every member of the family − from ten-year-old grandson to ninety-year-old grandmother − to be part of the team − and to make their contribution on equal terms.

Now, of course, we, the two Davids, who used to get headlines because of our youth, are probably regarded as elder statesmen of the game. We still

think of ourselves as a couple of youngsters, but, in reality, we are more often opposed by pairs who are younger than we are than those who are older.

We've been together now for twenty-five years! And, in that time, we've seen a lot of changes. But nothing that we have seen has lessened our love for the game — and we are still as enthusiastic about it as we were in 1965 — our first season together.

Since we struck up a partnership our careers in bowls have taken us all around the world, and given us opportunities that would never have come our way as schoolteachers. In this round-up of our

Older and wiser, the authors (DRJ on left, DJB on right) are still in partnership after first teaming up in 1965.

career development, as in other parts of the book, we will get over the difficulty of having the same given name by referring to ourselves as DJB and DRJ.

EARLY DAYS
DJB

My earliest attempts to play bowls were made as soon as my hands were big enough to handle lawn bowls — not the miniature carpet bowls that we see today, but actual woods that were smaller than the real thing and designed for social roll-ups on the lawn. Father had acquired them from the green-keeper at Exmouth, I believe.

Not that we had an enormous house, or a lawn that resembled a bowling green — but the set-up was sufficient for me, at the age of seven or eight, to feel I was playing bowls! Often I would be joined by schoolfriends for a game of pairs or triples. We would use a golf ball as a jack.

The lawn bowls were supplemented by a set of croquet balls, which of course had no bias, but the camber on the lawn had the effect of bias, and, without knowing it, I must have learnt a lot about the physics of the game — bias, weight, angles and impact — that I put into practice today.

My route home from school took me past the bowling green, and I used to stop for half an hour or three quarters to watch them play. Mother knew where I was and didn't worry, and eventually I would saunter home for tea.

I fell in love with the game from the start. I suppose you could say it's in my blood. Although I played a lot of other sports — I was at one time a promising goalkeeper — it was always bowls I came back to.

In those days you had to be sixteen to join my father's club, the 'top club' as it used to be called in Clevedon — not merely because it was at the top of Chapel Hill! So, at first, I had to settle for a season ticket at Clevedon Promenade and a few unofficial games at Clevedon, often on a Captain's Day, or

when the visitors were short of a player.

I used to use Father's bowls — old lignums, and 5³⁄₁₆″ — and was always praying that someone wouldn't turn up so I could have a game of bowls. It amazes me now that, at ten or eleven I could manage the biggest bowl of the lot – 5³⁄₁₆″ is a size bigger than the maximum size 7 permitted today!

When I was thirteen, we heard there was a lad of similar age playing at West Backwell, only seven or eight miles from Clevedon, and the club members dreamt up the idea of a challenge between us, and put up so much money each. I beat Roger Harris by about four shots I believe, won five shillings, and found a new friend.

As soon as I had attained my sixteenth birthday, I became a member of Clevedon, which is still my home club. Roger decided to join Clevedon, and we struck up a partnership that took us to the Somerset pairs championship in 1953 and 1957, and to the England final in 1959.

To emphasize the family aspect of the game, Roger's father and mine, Len Harris and Reg Bryant, joined forces with us to compete in the fours, and, in 1957, we won the English title at Paddington — and I received the first of my sixteen English Bowls Association (EBA) gold medals.

That, of course, was after I had taken time off, so to speak, first on national service, then as a trainee teacher at Cheltenham. I was lucky enough to get a post at Highdale junior school in Clevedon, back in the bosom of my family, and in the place I had been brought up.

There is something about Clevedon that I love. Having spent a few brief years in Bristol in the 1970s, I was relieved to return to the town that I feel comfortable in. My success owes a great deal to my settled home life, to the support of my wife, Ruth, and perhaps the quiet discipline of teaching in a small town helped to establish my (relatively) placid temperament.

DRJ

Like DJB, I've never known a time when I wasn't absorbed in the game of bowls. But, while he started with lawn bowls, I learnt the basics using marbles — in the 'passage' of our end-of-terrace Llanelli (it was Llanelly in those days) home.

The carpet sloped, so the run of the marble swung just like a bowl on a green. True, you could only use one hand, but, to me, the effect was electrifying. My disbelief totally suspended, I was transported in my mind to the finals green in the Welsh championships — and would play the part of both competitors.

Though I enjoyed the thrill of the take-out shot even in those days, I learnt that the draw was the most effective shot in the game — and I gave myself as many goes as it took to save the match with a perfect draw. All right, it was cheating on a sizeable scale — but it was a wonderful lesson in weight control!

My father, Charles, was a keen bowler, and a respected skip with the Ty'rfran club in Parc

DRJ (*far left*) started a bowls team at Caerleon Teachers' Training College in 1961. His happy fellow-students were (*l-r*) Quintin Lewis, David Evans and Derek Jones.

Howard. Ty'rfran means 'the House of the Crow', and, from the age of four or so, I used to perch at the end of his rink, like a bird of prey, keeping the score and taking it all in.

I attended Llanelli Grammar School, and tried the usual sports. I'd have given my right arm to have played Rugby, of course, but I suppose I wouldn't have been awfully useful with one arm. I made a reasonable off-side wing forward, and as a cricketer my forward defensive stroke wasn't too bad — but I always felt that bowls was the game for me . . . it was *my* game!

My father was not keen on my taking up bowls at such an early age, and the lower age limit for joining a club and playing in tournaments was then eighteen. So it was to his horror that I started playing 'illegally' for a local works team, Llanelly Steel, where one of my fellow novices was David Richards, now a Welsh selector.

It was a great team to play with, very friendly, yet competitive, and there were several old characters at skip who commanded respect and from whom I learnt a lot about tactics — especially the old adage, 'If you can't get the shot, make sure you get a good second.'

There were lots of youngsters playing then, and I remember reaching the final of an Under 18 event at Burry Port in 1958. It is not completely true that youth in bowls is a new phenomenon. Several of my schoolfriends used to while away the summer holidays in People's Park with an afternoon challenge in the sun. Yes, it was always sunny in those days.

When I was eighteen, I left the town for college in Caerleon, near Newport, where I started a bowls team, insisting, as College President, that full College colours were awarded for members of the team. We played at any club that would have us — on condition that they had a bar — and a good time was had by all.

The following year, I caught the eye of the Welsh selectors, who put me in the Welsh Under 35 side to play England at Ebbw Vale. When, later, I took up a teaching post in England and joined the Clevedon club, I kept very quiet about my Welsh 'cap' — until well after I had been selected to play for England in 1970.

At my interview for the post at Gordano School in Portishead, where I taught for twenty-two years, my fanaticism for the game of bowls revealed itself when I was asked the traditional question, 'Well, Mr Rhys Jones, have you anything you would like to ask us?'

'Are there any bowling clubs around here?' was my immediate response. Surprisingly, I got the job! Actually, one of the school governors was able to inform me there was a club at Clevedon, some five miles down the road. 'Clevedon . . . Clevedon . . .', I thought. 'Isn't that where that famous, up-and-coming bowler comes from?' (DJB had just returned from Perth, Australia, after winning his first Commonwealth Games gold medal.)

'Wouldn't it be nice if I could join that club . . . I might meet him, and possibly play with or against him some time . . .' It was a dream that was going to come true . . . and in a way I couldn't possibly have imagined.

1 GETTING STARTED

WHY PLAY BOWLS?

Ask any bowler why he plays the game, and he'll probably have to stop and think. That's because there are so many reasons, and so many benefits from the game, that he's probably not sure where to start.

There are those who take up the game for purely social reasons. They regard the bowls club as a place to meet people, and perhaps to while away their retirement in congenial company. They generally find what they are looking for. And they rarely ask for anything more.

Then there are many who, once they have given up the more physically demanding sports of their youth, seek to take exercise, and see in bowls an ideal, not-too-strenuous activity which will challenge them without over-stretching their diminishing physical capacity.

And there are, perhaps more commonly these days, those who are attracted by the challenge of big-money prizes now that the game of bowls has moved into an era of sponsorship and high-profile television coverage.

Both of us represent the relatively small but growing percentage of people who were introduced to bowls in their youth, and took immediately to the simplicity of the game that makes demands on hand-and-eye co-ordination and the individual's powers of concentration.

Funnily enough, neither of us sees himself as belonging to the category of pot-hunter suggested by the third group described above. True, we have had success on the green, and that success has benefited us financially in different ways – DJB as a player and consultant, DRJ as a journalist and commentator. But we both play bowls for the fun of it.

Of course, the 'fun of it' includes all sorts of things: the satisfaction of bowling a dead-length toucher; the excitement of killing an end when six shots down; the thrill of winning a good match, or a prestigious championship; the enjoyment of playing sport on grass, in the open air, with the sun on your back – or on a perfect indoor surface in the warm, on a cold, British winter's day; the aesthetic beauty of watching a bowl bend gracefully towards the jack; and, perhaps above all, the genuine sport ing friendship, camaraderie, rapport and repartee of a well-contested team-game.

Whatever reason you may have (or may have had) for starting to play bowls, you are guaranteed to experience all of those qualities – and more – even if the thought of playing competitive bowls was not really uppermost in your mind when you set out to join a club.

Many is the novice who has proved to have more aptitude than he thought he would. So, don't be shy. Have a go. And, although there is nothing wrong with playing bowls for entirely social reasons, do not be afraid of advancing if you find you have the natural ability.

Bowls, you see, is different from most sports. Being a stance sport, it gives priority to skill rather than speed or strength. Your reactions **Bowls gives priority to skill rather** do not have to be lightning-fast – you **than speed or strength** just have to have a good eye. So, many people who thought they weren't any good at sport, find they can manage bowls very well, because there is nothing wrong with their basic co-ordination skills.

We often say that good ball-players make excellent bowlers. They certainly tend to transfer the skills they have learnt at soccer, cricket or Rugby football very quickly. But co-ordination, a good eye and determination may also be the gift of a non-athletic person. Indeed, handicapped people can and do turn their hand to bowls with great skill.

If you have the natural ability, the sky's the limit − and you won't know whether you have the special skill it takes to be good at bowls until you've tried. But, whether you turn out to be a social or a competitive bowler, we are certain you will find riches in the game you never dreamed were there.

Perhaps we should express our basic dislike of the traditional demarcation between social and competitive bowlers. In our experience, so-called social bowlers can be extremely competitive − only masochists actually like losing − and we have found the top competitive bowlers to be among the most sociable all over the world.

JOINING A CLUB

Once you have decided to have a go at bowls, you should approach a club in your locality. Bowlers are a friendly breed, and will be glad to help with advice. Unfortunately, these days, a lot of clubs have a full membership, but that is simply a sign that the game is gaining in popularity all the time.

Sometimes, waiting lists are as long as your arm, and the best advice you can then get is a recommendation to approach another club. In the meantime, you would be well advised to get in some practice, which is a lot easier outdoors in the summer than indoors in the winter months.

Many private clubs have open days, and others may have an introductory scheme which will enable you to enjoy a friendly roll-up without obligation. You certainly don't want to join a club before you know whether or not you are going to like the game. It is sometimes difficult for an outsider to approach a private club, however, and a public or parks green may be a more straightforward proposition.

You see, there are all sorts of clubs, because over the years they have been formed in so many different ways to suit so many kinds of people. Basically, though, they fall into three categories: **Parks clubs,** who play on public greens − provided as a leisure amenity by the local authority; **works clubs** that play on greens that have been provided by firms as a recreation facility for their employees; and **private clubs**, whose membership generally own the premises and green, and run the club as a small business.

The same distinction applies indoors, too, except that there are few indoor clubs run by industrial firms and companies. Generally, indoor clubs are run either by the local leisure services department (often as part of the town sports centre) or by a private concern (perhaps a business venture, or possibly as the indoor section of an outdoor club).

Parks clubs often lease the premises from the local council, who are responsible for the upkeep of the green. They often seek permission to build their own clubhouse and pavilion, and more and more parks clubs are tending to install their own bar. Many are beginning to resemble private clubs − indeed, you could say that a lot of them are now private clubs that operate on public greens.

MEMBERSHIP FEES

With the increasing costs of upkeep and green maintenance, the price of outdoor season tickets for the general public on a parks green is often more expensive than at a private club − especially a private works club that might well be subsidized by the firm.

On a public green, of course, the beginner does not have to join the club before he can play − indeed, he doesn't have to join a club at all. Normally at least one, and often two rinks are kept available for casual play, which means that members of the general public − the community charge payers! − can hire the facility and enjoy a friendly roll-up.

The club has use of the other four or five rinks, and all club members will have a season ticket. The parks club, of course, has to surcharge its members to build up its own funds, and to pay its affiliation fees to the appropriate associations – at both county and national level.

Recently, the cost of belonging to the Clevedon promenade club (who play on a Woodspring District Council green) rose so steadily that, at £49.40 (including season ticket), it stood higher than the £35 plus VAT subscription that the prestigious Clevedon club (private, of course) asks of its members, prompting Clevedon to increase its annual fee to a more realistic £50 plus VAT.

In different parts of England, fees may vary, just like the price of a season ticket, but at the time of writing our examples are representative enough of the sort of fees you may be expected to pay at parks or private clubs.

One thing which seems standard: outdoor membership fees almost always include **green fees**. So you can have an unlimited amount of play for no extra outlay. We remember a time when every visitor made a contribution to the greenkeeper's fund – a kind of gratuity to eke out his paltry salary. There are fewer greenkeepers as such these days – greens tend to be looked after by consortiums of maintenance contractors – so the tradition of sixpence for the greenkeeper has fallen by the wayside, as has the quality of a lot of our greens. We wonder if there is any connection!

Indoors, though you play for a longer period in the year (September to April as a rule), the annual subscription is usually considerably smaller. Clevedon, for example, asks a mere £10 from its indoor members, while Bristol pitches its indoor membership at £19.

But, because green space is in such great demand, and because indoor bowls must be run on a businesslike footing, you pay a green fee every time you use the green. Sessions must usually be booked in advance, and a lot of the time the green is in use for league play morning, afternoon and evening.

A session normally lasts two hours, so leagues have to be played to a time limit (eighteen ends or two hours is a common format). For league play, each player pays between 80p and £2 per session, according to the club, which, with eight players on each rink, amounts to anything between £6.40 and £16 per rink per session. What, then, would be your total expenditure for a winter season of indoor bowls? Each league involves something like thirty matches, of which any individual might expect to play twenty (six players in a team putting four on the green for each match is the norm). You might play in two weekly leagues, so you might notch up forty matches through the winter. Add another ten matches for national and county competitions, and, say, another ten for club friendlies, and that makes sixty appearances over eight months — two games a week.

Club membership fee £19
60 games @ £1.10 ....£66
TOTAL...............................£85

Not bad for a winter's entertainment, but don't forget that you will have to add the cost of petrol or bus fares and the traditional lubrication — non-alcoholic of course, if you're driving — for you and your opponent. Still a bargain, though, surely.

If you enter the national indoor championships, the time limit aspect is not acceptable, so even for singles, the home player must book the rink for two two-hour sessions. Many clubs recognize the importance of these national championships by making a price concession, charging, perhaps, a nominal £2 per player per session, regardless of whether it's singles, pairs, triples or fours.

COACHING

Every new bowler deserves to be introduced to the game properly, but, surprisingly, until recently, newcomers have been left to their own devices — or bombarded with confusing advice from a host of people who are hardly qualified to give it.

In golf, it is usual for a beginner to have his or her action pass muster before being allowed on the main course. And it is the respected club professional who is responsible for getting the novice into shape. That is exactly what is needed in bowls, and we are glad to say that, in England at any rate, there are moves in that direction.

The English Bowls Coaching Scheme (EBCS) has been in existence since 1980, founded by someone whom we have known and respected for many, many years. Jimmy Davidson was England's singles champion in 1969, and has been a major influence on the game of bowls as we know it today.

DJB remembers skipping against Jimmy in the mid-Sixties, when, in a Somerset v Hampshire Middleton Cup quarter final, Peter Line was Jimmy's third man and DRJ his opposite number. Peter is now the national coach for the southern region, and DRJ is the video producer for the EBCS.

Gwyn John, a rugged Welshman who lives in Bude on Cornwall's Atlantic coast, has now succeeded Jimmy as National Coaching Director, but continues to proclaim the same message – the need to help every newcomer to adopt an error-free delivery – and aims to establish a qualified bowls coach in every club in the land.

It is appropriate here for us as joint authors to give our separate views on coaching, arrived at from two different perspectives. Neither of us was coached as a youngster; both of us have arrived at our own deliveries in our own way; but we are both firm believers in the value of good coaching.

DRJ

I subscribe to the opinion that, because people are different, they should be treated as individuals. Every person is unique in terms of stature, physique, suppleness and general state of fitness. Just as the size of hands influence the choice of bowls, so the other factors should shape a delivery that is unique to the player.

The modern EBCS method of introducing a beginner to the game of bowls is therefore very open-ended. What is natural is best – and what is

Gwyn John, England's National Director of Coaching, gives instruction to a young hopeful.
(*Duncan Cubitt/ Bowls International Magazine*)

comfortable is probably natural. Coaches can often help a beginner find the most natural delivery for him or her, but you will never find an EBCS coach starting a session by saying 'This is the way to hold a bowl . . .'

Imagine the confusion that would result in the beginner's mind if he were bombarded with instructions: Grip the bowl like this; stand like that; shorten your step; lengthen your backswing; spread your fingers; watch those feet; look at the shoulder; don't lift your head; careful you don't foot-fault etc!

Bowls is all about rolling a ball — something everyone can do. They can see if they are rolling it too far, or not far enough, too far to the left, or too far to the right. The movement, then, is a natural one, and the correction of mistakes a simple matter of intelligence. The coach should not have too much to say about it.

Bowls is all about rolling a ball — something everyone can do

Of course, if a bowler is not achieving a consistent action, the coach can guide and cajole him; if there is a bump in the delivery, the coach can suggest ways of eliminating it; if the beginner's style is too complicated, the coach can help him to keep it simple.

Every club should have a coach. That's for sure. If the club you approach doesn't have one ten years after the EBCS was born, find another club! But don't expect the coach to do everything for you. That's not the style today, I'm glad to say.

DJB

I may seem a strange advocate of coaching, having never been coached in my life. Right from the start, I developed my own style, and there has never been a time when I didn't analyse everything I did — for myself.

Some people say I'm a natural — and I suppose in a way I am. But, although I took to bowls like a duck to water, I have never been content to allow nature to take over to the extent of doing things without thinking.

Too many 'naturals', brilliant on their day, have nothing to fall back on when their talent lets them down. I believe you have to be able to provide an emergency service for the occasions when the wheels fall off.

Too many 'naturals', brilliant on their day, have nothing to fall back on when their talent lets them down

You have to have a good grounding in technique to do this, and coaching is an essential part of the process.

I have, I suppose, been my own coach. I have taken my delivery to pieces and put it back again, and I am always looking for ways to improve my technique. Because there were no coaches when I started, I've had to do it all myself, and now I feel quite confident that I can diagnose any faults and put them right.

Perhaps, to be honest, it is easier for me because I know exactly what I am doing. I keep my delivery very tightly controlled, and am, therefore, never likely to have more than one fault developing at any one time. It's like keeping a car well serviced — it may seem a bit of a bind at the time, but it's well worth it in the long run.

Someone whose delivery is not so well-serviced might be suffering from several faults at the same time, and it would be very difficult even for an experienced coach to spot what is going wrong. For the bowler himself it would be impossible.

My visits to Australia have taught me a lot about coaching. Perhaps the Aussie system is a bit regimented, but the speed of the greens in the southern hemisphere makes it essential to have a controlled delivery. Australian coaching methods are very highly developed, and are well explained in a video film called *In the Groove* (see Chapter 8).

Dropping the back knee is a vital part of the action, as well as shortening the backswing and slowing down all movement. As a result, nearly all Australian bowlers have the same action, which may not be an entirely good thing, but I can speak of the standard down under, which is generally very high indeed − real strength in depth.

Certainly the thing I would copy from the Australians is the process whereby every beginner has to have his or her delivery passed by the coach before being allowed to play on the main greens.

At the time of writing, I am embarking on an exciting venture at a huge coaching centre called Quietwaters in Essex. The golf coaching will be supervised by David Leadbetter, tennis by Mark Cox, and I will be setting up a brand new coaching scheme for bowls.

I hope to be able to pass on my experience of a whole variety of techniques, most of which I have tried and tested in competition all over the world in all sorts of playing conditions. And there are several other styles of delivery that I have not used myself but which I consider to have their own value − like the South African clinic style advocated by Dr Julius Serge.

I would say there is a lot to be said for keeping things simple, but my own delivery is often described as being complicated. It really isn't as complicated as it looks, and there is, I assure you, a reason for every aspect of my action. I could justify every movement − but I would not go as far as to say that my delivery would suit everyone.

My advice to a beginner would be to try a number of different styles before settling for the most comfortable, try to keep it simple, but, above all, think about everything you do. That's how I started − and I'm still rethinking my delivery all the time. You're never too old to learn.

2 EQUIPMENT

The most important purchase for a beginner is when he or she chooses a set of bowls. Too often the decision is made too early, without proper consideration. We have even heard of people receiving a set of bowls chosen from a catalogue by a well-meaning but non-bowling relative, and given as a birthday or Christmas present before the novice has even joined a club.

Your set of bowls is an investment Your set of bowls is an investment. Think how a snooker player feels about his cue, a golfer about his favourite putter, or a cricketer about his bat. One of the authors is a keen fisherman, whose rod is not so much an instrument for catching fish, but more a trusty friend.

DJB has several sets of bowls:
I chose them all very carefully for use on different surfaces and different conditions, and all of them fit comfortably into my hand, and slip beautifully away, hopefully on the right line. I know them through and through. They are all size 6, but represent a whole range of bias from wide swing to straight.

DRJ has only one set:
I have one set, and one set only. I don't feel able to cope with the constant dilemma of making a choice as to which set to use every time I take to the green. The set, average bias, 5$\frac{1}{16}$" diameter (size 6), no grips, just couldn't be simpler, but has served me

well for nearly thirty years, and given good value for the £12.17s.6d they cost me in 1964.

WHAT IS AVAILABLE?

How should you go about choosing the right bowl for you? Let us first consider the variables — the choices you will be asked to make.

MAKE

Bowls are produced by a number of manufacturers world-wide. The one which makes more bowls than anyone else is the Australian firm, Henselite, founded by William D. Hensell in 1918 and still run

Take your time choosing a set of bowls. A comfortable grip is what you are looking for. *(David Rhys Jones)*

by members of the famous bowling family. Britain's most popular bowl is made by another family firm, Thomas Taylor — Noel Taylor is still in charge of the company formed by his great great grandfather, James Taylor, in 1796.

SIZE

Bowls come in nine different sizes, from the smallest, size 00 (meant for children or people with extremely small hands) up to size 7, which is 5⅛" (13cm) in diameter. They used to manufacture bowls with a 5³⁄₁₆" diameter, but that was when woods were still made from wood.

BIAS

It has never been possible for a bowler to specify an exact degree of bias when he purchases a new set of bowls. There are technical reasons for this which are too difficult to explain here. But there have, regrettably, been pressures to introduce minimum biased bowls over the past few years, and one manufacturer now gives a choice between outdoor and indoor models.

COLOUR

Bowls are available in brown or black, with some variation in hue in the brown range. We have seen bowls that were almost orange in colour, and others with a green tinge, but most are what we would call mahogany.

GRIPS

It is necessary to distinguish between the terms **grip** and **grips**. Some bowls have a good 'grip'. They are made of a substance that feels secure in the hand. The old Dunlop bowls contained a relatively high percentage of rubber in their composition, for example, and Henselite introduced a composition called 'Super-Grip' in 1959.

'Grips' are different. They are markings, normally around the side of the bowl — hatching or patterning, or fairly deep dimples, intended to give the fingers something to grip. Most manufacturers now offer bowls with or without such grips.

EMBLEMS

Most people, thanks to television, realize that the small disc indicates the bias-side of the bowl, and the phrase, 'Big ring on the outside!' is a popular catch-phrase with bowlers everywhere. It is inside these discs that you can expect to see an emblem, or perhaps the initials of the owner of the set of bowls. You can order a set of new bowls with or without such identification marks.

CHOOSING THE RIGHT BOWLS FOR YOU
SIZE

The most basic thing to consider is the size of the bowl, and the size of your hand is the controlling factor. But, unfortunately, there is no easy way of measuring exactly what size bowl is right for you. In practice, comfort is far more impor- **Comfort is far more important** tant than theory, and the gauges that **than theory** are supposed to measure your hand and come up with the appropriate size for you should be taken with a pinch of salt.

If you can hold the bowl comfortably, try turning your hand upside down. If the bowl still feels secure and does not drop on your toe, it is certainly not too big! We have a club colleague in Clevedon who uses a size 7. She has a smallish hand, but is one of the best women bowlers in the area and a former winner of the English triples championship.

GRIPS

Choose the biggest bowl you can manage — but remember that under certain conditions, like wet or cold weather or extreme heat, you may experience problems with your grip. That is where the optional grips may be a good idea. Neither of the authors have ever used grips, because they were not an option when we started our bowling careers, but we do recommend that you consider their value.

MAKE

Choose a popular make. We do not give this advice to increase the profit margins of the leading manufacturers, but because it makes sense. Henselite and Thomas Taylor have been in the business for a very long time. They know what they are doing, and you won't go far wrong using their products. It's just not worth experimenting with untried makes.

BIAS

Perhaps the most important advice of all would be to urge the beginner to resist the temptation to choose straight bowls. Bowls is all about bias: learning to judge the amount of swing to bring the bowl back to the jack. And the joy of bowls is to watch that aesthetic curve that allows your wood to get around the short bowls that look in the way.

If there is one unnatural thing about bowls it is having to roll a ball in one direction when you want it to finish in another. Giving it green is the thing you have to learn above all others. And a bowl with narrow bias does not encourage you to give green; indeed, it encourages you to cut the green and keep it tight.

Choose, if you can, a bowl with generous bias. Quite apart from the incentive to play bowls properly and set your bowl on a wide arc, a stronger bias allows a greater variety of shots to be played. As you will see later, using a range of heavy shots enables you to enter the head at a variety of angles, and there are more options available.

All bowls, if they are legal, have to bend at least as much as the Master Bowl, a copy of which is kept by all the authorized testers throughout the world. Rather confusingly, all legal bowls are designated Number Three bias, and there is a wide range within that title. So it will not help you to order a Number Three bias — and most non-specialist dealers will have no idea of what bias they are selling you.

Henselite are moving towards offering a choice between indoor and outdoor models, and have designed the indoor bowls with a weaker (narrower) bias. This meets a demand from some British bowlers who would like to bowl indoors in conditions nearer to playing on grass, where – in Britain at least — there is less swing because the greens are heavier.

Remember that, although the manufacturer makes a distinction between indoor and outdoor models, they are actually interchangeable in practice. You can use your indoor bowls outdoors, and your outdoor ones on carpet — as long as they are properly stamped according to the laws of the appropriate ruling body. Those laws are so complicated that they are best left to the bowls legislators. They won't worry you until you qualify to play in a national championship final.

There is a lot to be said for borrowing a set of bowls at first, if you can. Try several different ones — sizes, makes and biases. Then make up your mind which you prefer and visit a specialist dealer, who knows what he is talking about. If he can't guarantee you the kind of bowl you are looking for, you may be better off hunting in the second-hand market.

For a new set of bowls you could expect to pay up to £130, while a set of second-hand woods can be picked up for around £50 or so. If you go for a used set, ask if you can try them out first. Most bowlers would be pleased to agree.

CLOTHING

There are plenty of mail order firms who specialize in bowls clothing. Shoes are probably the most important purchase, as comfort is vital. While white shoes are becoming more acceptable, it would be as well to enquire about the local domestic rulings before buying a pair. Some clubs and associations still forbid white shoes, and insist on brown.

The other items of clothing will be dictated by the club you join. They will probably expect you to equip yourself with a blazer, perhaps with the club badge. White trousers or skirts, with white also above the waist, is now standard for everything apart from friendly roll-ups, and in some clubs even for those.

Waterproofs are, sadly, a necessity in the United Kingdom. Don't make the mistake of buying a cheap pair. Try to get a pair with plenty of room inside, to give you freedom of movement — and make sure you put them away carefully after use. Too many waterproofs are ruined by being put away wet. Hang them up to dry before folding them.

EQUIPMENT

Every bowler likes to possess a **measure**. You don't know when you will be invited to play third, and

An up-to-date rule book is a must for anyone who intends to take the game at all seriously

beginners can learn a lot about the game by marking singles ties. A good pair of callipers, obtainable at any hardware store, is also a good idea, though few bowlers seem to have one. Make sure you get well acquainted with the rules — an up-to-date **rule**

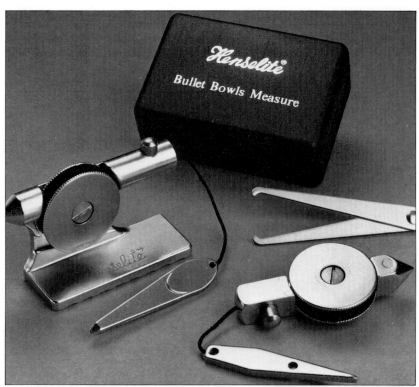

There are many pieces of equipment available including measures and callipers, which are of value to all players. Many players swear by Grippo, a wax which assists their grip.
(Courtesy of Henselite)

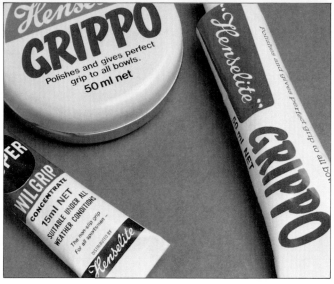

book is a must for anyone who intends to take the game at all seriously.

If you have problems holding your woods in the wet, there are several brands of **wax** on the market that can assist your grip. One of the oldest is called Grippo, and many people swear by it. Feelings are divided, however. One of the authors uses the stuff liberally, even in the dry; the other doesn't touch it at all.

A **duster** or chamois leather might be all that is necessary to dry the wood before you grip it, and there are some bowlers who carry a duster with them everywhere — Tony Allcock uses one indoors, as everyone who has watched him in action on the portable rink will be aware.

Apart from a piece of **chalk** for marking touchers, that's all the equipment you are likely to need, because all the bigger items are provided by the club. Unlike crown green, you won't need your own jack, and the mats come as standard equipment on every bowling green.

3 THE LANGUAGE OF THE GAME

BACK BOWL
A bowl deliberately or otherwise placed behind the jack (i.e. between the jack and the ditch). It is often very valuable to have the best back bowl, in case the jack finds its way to the back of the rink or into the ditch.

BOWLS
Bowls are known as woods, because they were once made from Lignum Vitae ('wood of life'). Now they are moulded from a composition of phenol formaldehyde powder. But we still hear of good woods, bad woods, back woods, narrow woods, wide woods and second woods.

DEAD END, BURNT END OR KILLED END
When the jack is driven out of bounds, the end is said to have been burnt or killed. The end will be replayed, and will not be recorded as a played end. There is sometimes a penalty for killing an end in domestic play − but never in the proper game. It is an accepted part of the game.

DRAWING
The art of getting your bowl to finish near the jack (or other object). Using exactly the right weight for the job − no more and no less!

FIRING OR DRIVING
A desperate, destructive shot which aims to clear as many of the opponent's shots away from the jack, or to kill the end by putting the jack off the rink.

Occasionally used more positively to take out a single bowl to score a count. Look for the danger before driving.

FOREHAND AND BACKHAND

Forehand sees the bias bring the bowl back from right to left, while a backhand delivery swings the bowl from left to right — as far as a right-hander is concerned! Forehand is the same as finger-peg, while backhand corresponds to thumb-peg in crown green parlance.

FULL HOUSE OR PAN-FULL

The rare achievement of scoring with all your team's bowls on one end. A count of four in singles is relatively common, but an eight in fours is very rare indeed.

HEAD

The cluster of bowls around the jack is called the head. No two heads develop in exactly the same way — that is the beauty of the game of bowls.

JACK

The little white ball is variously known as the jack, the kitty, the kate, the cot, the pot or the white, according to where you live. Now that a yellow jack has been introduced for television, perhaps the white should become the yellow.

POLICEMAN OR BLOCK

A bowl deliberately placed in the track to the jack that the opponent would like to use. It guards or protects, often against an anticipated firing shot. A very difficult shot to play.

REST

Using the opponent's bowls in the head is quite an art. If he has a bowl close to the jack, you can make use of it. Using slightly more than drawing weight, your bowl can rest against your opponent's, and take the shot.

SPLIT

Two bowls close together but not touching each other offer an inviting target. A weighted bowl accurately homing in on the gap between the bowls will part them and stay around in a usefully predictable position.

TIED END

When the two bowls nearest to the jack belong to opposite sides and are found to be equidistant — perhaps both touching the jack — the end is said to be tied, and no score is recorded. The end, however, has been legitimately played, and the occurrence is recorded on the scorecard as 0 shots to each side.

TOUCHER

A bowl that touches the jack in its original course is a toucher, and remains a live bowl, even if it falls into the ditch.

TRAILING

A skilful shot that involves picking the jack up and moving it perhaps towards a cluster of your team's bowls. A level green jack will often stay with the trailing wood, unlike a crown green jack that will normally stop the running bowl in its tracks.

WICK

A glancing blow which brings a wood (normally rather fortunately) into contention is called a wick. Not a very polite term.

WREST

Pronounced in the same way as rest, this shot uses more weight — enough to push an offending bowl out of the head and take its place, thus wresting the shot from your opponent.

WRONG BIAS

Take care to ensure that your bowl is correctly positioned in your hand — so that the heavier side (bias) will bring it back towards the jack, not on to the next rink. The bias side of the bowl, which will always be on the inside of the curve, can be identified as the side with the small disc. Ignore this advice, and you will bowl a wrong bias. You'll take some ribbing, and possibly be asked to stand a round of drinks!

YARD OF WEIGHT

A most misused term. An invitation from your skip to use a yard of weight should see you deliver your bowl with just enough weight to reach a point ONE YARD behind the jack or other target. Sometimes, alas, the response is more like a firing shot or drive.

4 THE GAME EXPLAINED

Bowls is becoming a spectator sport. The authors believe that some of the secrets of the game need revealing, so that uninitiated onlookers can understand what is going on. Bowls is a simple game, but sometimes the simple strategies — the what, why or how — need to be explained.

'What's he doing that for?' Perhaps that's a question which has occurred to you when watching bowls on television. Despite — perhaps even because of — the basic simplicity of the game, many people say they find it difficult to understand bowls.

There is a lot more to the game than trying to get your bowls as close as possible to the jack

There is, in fact, a lot more to the game than trying to get your bowls as close as possible to the little white ball called the jack. Make no mistake, however, the basis of the game is just that. For a start, scoring depends on you getting your bowls nearer to the jack than your opponent gets his.

But, although the game is simple, every end is unique, and every head develops in a different way. Every time a bowler stands on the mat, he has a decision to make, and a variety of options to choose from. Drawing to the jack is just one of them.

What he decides to do depends on many factors . . . the state of the game . . . the state of the head . . . and the state of his mind . . . as well as his confidence to play the shot . . . on that green . . . on the day. If he decides against drawing to the jack, his choice of shot will reflect whether he is prepared to attack or content to defend.

The whole cat-and-mouse game resembles a

game of chess, played on a green chess-board, 40 yards (36.5m) long. What options are open to the player on the mat? When should he attack, and when defend? And how? We will face the problems and dilemmas from the point of view of a singles player, but the same basic principles will apply in the team situation.

SCORING

The player who has the nearest bowl to the jack when the end has been completed (all eight bowls have been played) scores on that end. How many shots he is awarded depends on the number of bowls he has nearer to the jack than his opponent's nearest.

Should we attack or defend? What are the dangers?
(Maurice Sims)

GOING FOR SHOTS

It may seem, therefore, that a player should attempt to get all his four bowls near to the jack, with the intention of scoring a full house (four shots) every end. That would not be a wise move for several reasons.

Firstly, grouping all your bowls around the jack would set up a big target which your opponent would love to hit. When drawing to the jack, you should try to leave your bowls on the centre line of the rink. If you can do that, you may get away with piling in the shots, because you are offering your opponent a single bowl target, which he will not be confident of hitting every time.

Secondly, grouping your bowls in a cluster anywhere on the rink is dangerous because you run the risk of leaving your opponent with a good chance of moving the jack towards a cluster of his own. A singles player should always look out for the dangers of dropping a count to an adventurous opponent.

DRAWING

The basic shot in bowls will always be the drawing shot, normally to the jack, and that is what the beginner – and the experienced player – should practise more than anything else.

Even with the draw-shot, however, there is a choice, because, thanks to the bowl's bias, the

The drawing shot should be practised more than anything else

perfect draw may be achieved on the forehand or the backhand. Many bowlers, even at top level, have a preference for one or the other, but all successful bowlers will have mastered both forehand and backhand.

FOREHAND

Forehand, for the right-handed player, sees the bowl delivered on the right-hand side of the rink, requiring the bowl to swing, with the bias, back to the left, finishing, with luck, on the centre line of the rink, nestling close to the jack.

BACKHAND

Backhand, again for the right-handed player, sees the bowl delivered on the left-hand side of the rink, swinging back to the right to finish in the very same place.

WHAT'S THE DIFFERENCE?

There really is no difference at all between forehand and backhand. In each case, the player selects a line — a straight line — along which to launch the bowl; then watches as the inherent bias of the bowl brings his guided missile back to the centre of the rink.

There are factors, however, which make forehand and backhand appear to have different characteris-

The basic shot in bowls will always be the drawing shot. Every bowler dreams of achieving the dead-length toucher.
(Maurice Sims)

tics; and greens where one hand or the other will be best left well alone.

GROUNDING POINT

It will be obvious that the point of delivery — that is the point on the rink where the bowl is grounded — is not the same for forehand and backhand deliveries.

When using the forehand, the point of delivery will be on the right-hand side of the rink; when using the backhand, it will be on the left. And, normally, the forehand point of delivery will be further from the centre line of the rink than is the backhand point of delivery — simply because of the width of the body, and the use of the right hand.

A left-hander, on his forehand will, it follows naturally, ground the bowl further from the centre line on the left-hand side of the rink than his backhand grounding point is to the right of the centre line.

Because the forehand delivery starts the bowl on a comparatively wide position on the rink, the forehand shot, on a perfectly level green, seems to swing more than the backhand. Of course, it doesn't swing more at all — it's just the trajectory that is different.

VARIABLE GREENS

No green is ever perfect — and no green is ever truly level. Crown greens, of course, are not supposed to be — but greenkeepers tending 'level' greens are obviously expected to make them as level as they can. None of them has ever succeeded totally, and, over the world, their success rate varies a lot.

The best greens, outdoors, are in the southern hemisphere, where the climate allows the greenkeepers in New Zealand and Australia to achieve good levels and keep them that way. The greens are harder than British greens, and therefore less prone to a shifting of levels, and, of course, a lot faster, too.

Almost every rink has a discrepancy between one hand and the other. Experienced bowlers will look out for this discrepancy during the trial ends, and will instantly label the sides of the rink. 'The straight hand looks tricky', a bowler may say to his team after the trial ends, 'but the swinger appears to be more reliable.'

Wear is another factor that can cause trouble on a rink. Some parts are stood on for long periods, other areas are walked on constantly, and the rolling of the woods themselves can also adversely affect the true running of the rink. All these factors, though they undoubtedly make the game more interesting, ensure that scientific theory has only limited application.

So, there are many variables that make even the simple, straightforward draw-shot more difficult than it should be. A bowl that finishes some distance away from the jack may be intended as a positional bowl — or it may be a draw that failed. In the description that follows, it is assumed that the green or rink is perfect. In reality, it will never be so.

FORWARD IMPETUS AND SIDEWAYS PULL

The bowl is not round. Its irregular shape gives it the quality of bias. So, as the forward momentum imparted by the bowler decreases through friction between the running surface and the ground (grass or carpet) the sideways pull of the bias is allowed to have more and more influence.

That is why the bowl, as it leaves the hand, appears at first to travel more or less in a straight line, and why, as it slows down, it departs from that straight line and curves ever more steeply. The trick in drawing accurately is first to identify the line required and then dispatch the bowl safely and accurately in that direction. And at the right speed.

The more pace imparted to the bowl initially, the further it will travel before it starts to bend (although, strictly speaking, it actually bends from the moment it leaves the hand). It follows that it will also get further away from the centre line of the rink before it starts to bend. It will thus appear to have a wider draw.

But, although it goes further, the sideways pull of the bias will always bring the bowl back to the centre line of the rink — assuming that the identification of the 'correct' line, and the execution of the delivery have been in order.

Consequently, the line to bring the bowl back to the jack on the centre line will be the same whatever distance the jack may be from the mat. All that remains is for the bowler to judge the weight, pace or strength of the launch, so that his bowl will gently caress the jack.

Perhaps that makes the process seem complicated. It isn't really. Drawing is a simple matter of sending a bowl from point A to point B. And line and length are the only two commodities required to achieve this. Forget, for the moment, that the grass is uneven, that there may be a gusting crosswind, that the ground is not level. Forget the pressure of competition, and the consequences of failure.

Drawing is really the simplest shot in the book. Simple to understand; simple to theorize about; and simple to play. It really is a puzzle why even the top exponents don't get a dead-length toucher more often!

ATTACKING

There are times when a straightforward draw-shot is not the most appropriate response to the situation. Perhaps the track to the jack is blocked; **There are times when the draw-shot is not appropriate and an up-shot is called for** perhaps the accuracy demanded is simply too much to ask; perhaps the position is desperate; perhaps there is much to gain from trying to strike an opponent's bowl or move the jack.

On any of these occasions, an **up-shot** is called for. That's what they call it in New Zealand and Australia — and the phrase speaks for itself. In Britain, we have several different names for a variety of up-shots, each with a distinct aim in mind.

Every up-shot needs to be played with confidence, and it is important to have a thorough knowledge of the physics involved. Again it is a question of delivering from point A with point B in mind – but the bowl must still be moving, possibly quite quickly, when it reaches point B.

In simple terms, it is all a matter of cutting the angle, taking a narrower line, and increasing the weight. How it is done can be left until later, but it will be useful to refer to Chapter 7, and consider the recommended on-green practices for playing up-shots.

THE TAKE-OUT

Nothing to do with Chinese cuisine! The take-out is a firm shot, delivered with more than drawing weight, with the intention of removing an opponent's wood from the head. Perhaps it is his only saving wood, and its removal will net a valuable count.

THE SPLIT

The split is similar to the take-out, but involves contact with two bowls, not one. Two bowls usually offer a bigger target than one, and are therefore easier to hit, but more weight is needed to dislodge both of them. When the two bowls are positioned side-by-side, with a gap between them insufficient to allow a bowl to pass through, the shot is even more inviting.

Aiming to hit the gap, an accurate strike, splitting the two bowls, should leave the attacking bowl close to where the two bowls stood before. The attacking bowl will have been stunned by the double contact, and its limited onward movement is easy to predict. That is what makes the split such an inviting, profitable and popular shot. As a bonus, the enemy bowls have been summarily dispatched.

THE PROMOTION

Short bowls are not usually valued very highly, but when the way to the jack is blocked, it may be possible to make use of your own short bowls, and push them into a scoring position. Hitting a target the size of a bowl, or perhaps two bowls wide, is often easier than playing a perfect draw, because it may not be necessary to use precise weight to achieve the desired object.

There is a skill to the shot, however, for the relationship of line and length is still critical. The line is tighter (nearer to the centre line) than with a draw, and the pace correspondingly greater. It is not a matter of hurling the bowl and hoping for the best — a certain degree of finesse is required to achieve the optimum promotion.

THE TRAIL

The trail is the name given to a deliberate impact with the jack — the intention being to move the jack to a more advantageous position on the rink. The distance that the jack needs to be moved affects the judgement of pace: it may be that the trail should take the jack a matter of inches to a cluster of waiting bowls; there are times when the jack needs to be trailed several yards to the receiving back bowls.

Any shot that attacks the jack — with the intention of moving it — could be called a trail. Like the positive shot that ditched the jack and gave Scotland the gold medal in the fours at the Commonwealth Games at Auckland in 1990. Ian Bruce, playing two for the Scots, saw that his side had the advantage at the back, and went for the jack with enough weight to carry it right through to the ditch. Scotland scored four shots, and went into the last end six shots up. An excitingly decisive trail.

THE DRIVE OR FIRING SHOT

Everyone who has watched bowls will have seen an example of the drive or firing shot. It sends whispers of anticipation through the crowd, and sometimes murmurs of disapproval. It is the big gun — the destroyer. Used, more often than not, to negate the opponent's good work, to scatter his shot bowls, or maybe kill the end to earn a replay.

This is not the most subtle of shots, but it is a lot more difficult than it looks. A great deal of natural ability, together with diligent practice is needed to develop reliable and consistent accuracy under pressure — and, by definition, there is often a lot of pressure on when the big gun is brought out.

After all, the firer probably stands to lose a lot of shots if he misses — and sometimes he doesn't have a big target to hit. Someone like Australia's Rob Parrella, the 1990 Commonwealth Games champion, fires so accurately that he nominates which side of his target bowl he is going to hit — then hits it!

Such accuracy is pure skill, not, as some critics would have it, brute force. And it can be used in quite positive ways as well as destructively. Parrella, for example, often uses his dead-eye drive to take out a single bowl — and the effect can be quite devastating. Because of his use of extreme pace, he is virtually bound to lose his own bowl in the process, but he clearly finds it a more accurate way of making an extraction.

DEFENDING

Defensive play can be divided into two categories: attempting to keep what you've got; **Defend to keep what you've got and to** and trying to cut down the count, **restrict your opponent's score** restricting the opponent's score wherever possible.

INSURANCE — THE BACK BOWL

Applause is often heard for a bowl which finishes several yards/metres away from the jack. A wise player has played defensively, and has positioned a bowl where he considers the jack is likely to go if his opponent hits the head. Normally that means putting one round the back — because the jack rarely travels forwards, towards the mat.

Whether you are playing or spectating, make a habit of studying the head. Have a go at anticipating what each player is likely to play next. And try to predict what the consequences will be if the head is struck. Sometimes, the jack will move sideways, and occasionally even up the green. Choosing where a player needs a covering bowl is an interesting exercise.

The man holding shots can always take a calculated risk, ignore the danger and draw another shot. But he must be prepared to pay for the gamble. He may also decide not to put a bowl in the most likely place, but instead cover for the most damaging result.

MATCHING BOWLS

It may be crystal clear where the jack is likely to go, but only one shot may be lost in that area. It may be wiser to cover three enemy bowls in a position which does not seem a likely destination. Strange

things can and do happen in bowls, and it pays to cover for all eventualities if you can.

Matching the opponent's bowl is the traditional way of insuring against a big count. It may not make for spectacular bowls, but positioning each of your bowls carefully with due regard to the position of your opponent's previous delivery is good, solid defensive tactics.

THE POLICEMAN OR BLOCK

Putting in a back bowl is a way of cutting your losses if your opponent gets his shot. Putting in a block is your way of making his shot more difficult: trying to stop his shot rather than insuring against it.

You can never block all the shots – but a bowl on the centre line stops an all-out drive.
(*Maurice Sims*)

There are two snags. Firstly, the block shot is notoriously difficult to play. To be effective, it needs to be as precise as a dead-length toucher – inch-perfect! And, secondly, you can never block all the shots, merely cut down his options. A skilful opponent can always contrive a way to beat the block.

Imagine the block has been perfectly placed to stop a running bowl on the forehand. Using less weight, your opponent may be able to get round the rock; using more he may attack inside it, taking a narrower line. And there is always the backhand open to him. You may even force him into playing a shot he hadn't considered – and he might even get it!

Back bowls and blockers are used normally by a player who holds the shot and is satisfied with the head as it stands. They are often played in a relaxed manner, but are nonetheless important, and should be taken as seriously as any other shot in the book.

THE SECOND BOWL – THE SAVER

There is another kind of defensive bowl, played when the position is unfavourable. The head has built up badly, and you are uncomfortably aware of the prospects of dropping a big count. Your opponent has played the end well, but you have, perhaps, sailed through the head with your first three deliveries.

It is time for a disciplined approach. No consideration should be given to the possibility of trailing the jack through to those three inviting back bowls. An adventurous shot could, of course, turn three down into three up, but what if you missed? No! – yield not to temptation. It is time to play defensively. Draw a good second. Cut your losses. It's surprising how often you will be rewarded for such self-discipline by drawing, not the second, but the number-one shot!

This kind of shot, unglamorous as it is, wins matches, because it has a double effect – on the scoreboard and on your opponent. It prevents you dropping further behind than you absolutely have to — and it saps your opponent's confidence, as he realizes how difficult it will be to score a count against you.

THE DEFENSIVE DRIVE

It could be argued that, if the position in the head makes it impossible to draw even the second shot, a drive or firing shot is the best, perhaps only, option. The drive has already been described as an attacking shot, but, in a sense, it is also a means of defence. Anything that stops the rot, that cuts down the count, can clearly be regarded as defensive.

5 THE GAME FORMATS

Bowls is becoming a spectator sport. Television has recognized the qualities of our game and has done a good public relations exercise for bowls. It has kept all the good and traditional features of the game, and has kept innovations to a minimum. The few cosmetic improvements that have been made, have enhanced the game, making it more entertaining for the spectator without losing any of the intrinsic values.

Coloured shirts have been introduced; a new system of indicating the score has been developed, using 'lollipops'; games are now played on the sets system, though basic scoring remains unchanged: all these initiatives have made the game more accessible to the general public, who have been introduced to bowls mainly through watching singles play.

The Laws of the Game insist that 'the basis of the game of bowls is fours play', and singles is only a **The basis of the game of** small part of the game as a whole. But **bowls is fours play'** it is understandable why television prefers singles − classic head-to-head confrontation, and the general absence of clutter commend it to TV coverage and to spectators generally.

Anyone new to bowls, attracted perhaps by watching it on the small screen, needs to realize that club bowls revolves around fours play, and that pairs and triples are also popular with the punters. Singles may be the flag-ship of the sport, but there is a whole fleet following close behind, involving hundreds of thousands of club players in team events every day of the year.

Each format has its own qualities, which we hope to outline in the next few pages.

SINGLES

Each player in a game of singles is allowed four bowls, which he delivers alternately with his opponent, and the game, unlike team games, is played on a shots-up basis. British tradition has it that the first to score 21 shots is the winner, but things seem to be changing.

In the southern hemisphere, it was always accepted that singles should be played to 31 shots, until, in 1986, the International Bowling Board (IBB) decided that it should bring the two hemispheres together, and decreed that, at international level, singles games should be 25-up.

This idea has yet to find favour in the United Kingdom, where most national associations have stuck to the 21-up format, partly because the 25-up game could mean an extra eight ends, adding as much as half-an-hour to the average singles game.

The other 'new' system, which also has its opponents, is the sets format, which was devised for television. No-one doubts that the best-of-three or best-of-five 7-up sets format works well on the box. It produces more crises, more climaxes, and shorter game units, but few clubs have adopted sets for their own club championships.

DJB

I think the 25-up format is the best of all, because the longer game favours the better player. In my experience, the short, sharp bursts required by the sets system gives an advantage to the poorer player, because he is given an artificial incentive to concentrate — if he doesn't, he's out!

Mind you, I am a firm supporter of the sets system. I believe it's 100 per cent right for television. But, as far as pure bowls is concerned, I would go for the longer game every time. It's a real struggle to have to concentrate for perhaps thirty-five ends on the trot, without the dramatic structuring of sets

to help you — and I think you should be rewarded for mastering the art.

I like singles because I can shape my own destiny, and be my own boss. I can employ my own tactics, choose my own hand, and jack length, and play the game at my own pace. The other side of the same coin is that singles can be a lonely game, with no-one to share your troubles.

But, because you are bowling all the time, you can build up a rhythm, and get into a groove in a way which is impossible in team games. Concentration is in some ways easier, too, because, quite simply, you do not have anyone else to worry about.

It may surprise those who believe I am something of a singles specialist to learn that I was slow in taking to the solo game. I used to revel in team bowls, and, in fact, won five county titles in team events before I won my first county singles championship at the relatively advanced age of twenty-eight.

Opposite:
DJB is the acknowledged master of singles play. Apart from his phenomenal success in world championships, his greatest achievement was winning the BBC's Jack High Masters at Worthing nine times in the twelve years it was on offer.

DRJ

As a spectator, what I like about singles, is the confrontation and the conflict. Perhaps it's because I used to be a drama teacher, but I can always see so much more to the game than two men or women trying to get their bowls nearer to the jack than their opponents.

There is the physical side, it's true, but the tactical and psychological aspects are far more interesting. I love observing the body language of the players, spotting the one who thinks he's going to win, and the one who is under pressure. Watch out for the player who looks as if he owns the rink — he may suggest this with or without a display of arrogance, but he is the likely winner.

DJB, of course, has got the game of singles down to a fine art, and is better at dictating the pace of the game than anyone else. He is also a master at pulling the great shot out of the bag at exactly the right moment, though I don't believe even he knows how he is able to do this.

We all marvelled at how he was able to turn the game against David Corkill in the final of the 1989 CIS UK singles championship – playing a shot-in-a-million to save the match in the third set after losing the first two, and going on to clinch a miraculous victory.

He has now won the world singles championship six times (three times indoors, three times out), and the English singles nine times indoors, six times out. Between 1971 and 1973, he won the British outdoor singles title three times on the trot!

PAIRS

Two players in a side, each with four bowls, playing, normally, twenty-one ends. The first player, known as the lead, delivers his four, alternating with his opposite number, just like a game of singles, followed by the skip – so that there are sixteen bowls in the head by the time each end is complete.

If pairs is the most popular form of bowls, it is for two main reasons. Firstly, there is the company of a partner to share your triumphs and disasters, and, secondly, a continuity about the game, which keeps all four players involved all the time: when they are not delivering their bowls, they are directing the head, and giving their partner advice and support.

DJB and DRJ study an unusual head during the national indoor pairs championship in 1989.
(Duncan Cubitt/ Bowls International Magazine)

DJB

I like pairs, and feel it is popular because it is obviously easier to form a good pairs partnership at club level than it is to weld a good four together, partly for reasons of skill, and partly because it is

difficult to find four good players who can form a compatible unit.

The Australian version of pairs has always appealed to me, but it is an entirely different game. Each player still has four bowls, but the lead bowls

two of his (alternately with his opponent) before the skip bowls two of his. Then the lead plays another two, and the skip completes the end, playing his pair's last two bowls.

In New Zealand, they play yet another variation — with three bowls per player. On their fast greens, this means that the game can be finished in a reasonable amount of time.

DRJ

I have been privileged to lead for DJB in the national championships, indoors and out, for twenty-five years, and can also say that I have enjoyed every minute of it. But, I would like to correct a popular misconception that leading in pairs is exactly like playing a game of singles. It is not!

True, you have four bowls, and so does your opponent, but your prime objective is not to get the shot. You may often be trying to bowl to the jack, and you may happen to leave your skip lying shot or shots now and then — but that is not the aim of a good lead, nor the wish of his skip, who is more interested in position than shot.

If I concede the shot every end out of the twenty-one, I will still be happy if I have given my skip a favourable head to bowl at. After all, every skip worth his salt would expect to affect the head with at least one of his four bowls, and if I have got a good second and have put my other three bowls in a receiving position, I will feel I have played my part.

TRIPLES

Three players a side, playing three bowls each for eighteen ends. The fact that there are eighteen bowls in the head by the time the skips have finished means that there is often no way to get to the jack, and also that each end takes longer to play. That is why the number of ends required to produce a result is curtailed — compared with pairs and fours.

This form of team game was introduced to county

and national level competition in England as late as 1945, and has only recently grown in popularity. Now it is a common format for local open tournaments in England, often played on Sundays, when a festival atmosphere turns the club into a congenial meeting place — and battle-ground!

DJB

There is some confusion as to where the second man belongs in the triple. Does he stay at the mat end with the lead, or stand with the skip? I favour the latter, because it is much easier for him to spot the line to the jack from behind the head, from where he can watch the track taken by the leads. And, at the head, he can, of course, support and advise the skip and talk tactics more easily.

DRJ

Two-wood triples is played by devotees of the English Bowling Federation (EBF) in thirteen counties, mainly in the eastern part of England —

Two England players, Gary R. Smith (*left*) and Jim Lambert (*right*) flank their Stanley teammate, Richard McKie, with whom they won the national indoor triples title in 1990.
(Kevin Chevis/ Bowls International Magazine)

though, because they do not recognize fours, they like to call it rinks. We used the format at Clevedon for a Pro/Cel/Amateur event, and found it worked a treat.

Each triple consisted of a 'professional' bowler, a celebrity from the world of sport or entertainment, and a local amateur. The celebrities, most of whom were rolling a wood for the first time, were taught by the professionals, and coped very well on their bowls début. The two-wood format made each end a much more manageable unit of play.

FOURS

'The basis of the Game of Bowls is Fours play.' So say the Laws of the Game, and, indeed, this form of bowls is the most common for club matches —

friendlies, league or cup games — when each side is usually represented by four, five or six fours.

Members of a fours team are called lead, second, third and skip, and they play, of course, in that order, using two bowls each, and playing twenty-one ends — except when, in indoor leagues, for example, there may be a domestic ruling curtailing the match to, say, 'eighteen ends or two hours'.

DJB

I have always been surprised that fours is such a popular game, and that it is considered to be the basis of the game. At club level, I would have thought that pairs or triples would have offered more value in terms of participation — although, I suppose, the governing factor is getting as many as

Compatibility and team-work. The all-international Cyphers club quartet skipped by Andy Thomson (*second right*) are already the most successful four of all-time. Between 1983 and 1990, they won the English indoor title five times. (*l-r* Martyn Sekjer, Gary A. Smith, Andy Thomson, Terry Heppell)
(*Chris Mills/ Bowls International Magazine*)

forty-eight players on the green (six rinks, with eight on each) at a time.

One of the most difficult things about fours play is the long period of inactivity after you deliver your two bowls and before your turn comes round again. For the skip, it is not so bad, because he is, in a sense, playing *all* the bowls in every end, and is involved all the time – but for the lead, it is hard to keep concentrating.

In a fours game lasting four and a half hours (270 minutes) you can expect to go through your delivery only forty-two times, with gaps of 10 minutes between pairs of deliveries. Although it is easier to concentrate in singles, I would recommend every lead to enter singles competitions as good practice for drawing to the jack and as a way of monitoring his progress in the game.

Competing regularly at singles will also be a good test of temperament, and will indicate if the player has the potential to develop as a back-end player.

DRJ

While fours does seem to crowd the rink, and make for a drawn-out game, with attendant problems of concentration, there is a tremendous amount of satisfaction to be gained from being the member of a successful four – or part of a successful team. The camaraderie in England's international team is outstanding, and when four top players are in top gear, no-one complains about the long wait between bowls.

The answer seems to be in the continuous involvement of every player – even in the decision-making process. The humble lead or second should not be made to feel redundant once he has delivered his bowls. He should take an active interest in what happens next, give support to the three and skip, and be available for consultation.

Such team-work is not always a feature of fours play. Indeed, in many clubs, the lead and second are discouraged from venturing their opinions. Perhaps, admittedly, they should keep their comments to themselves if they tend to be carping or destructive, but they are members of the four, and should be given every opportunity to make a full and positive contribution.

POSITIONS AND RESPONSIBILITIES IN A FOUR

The lead bowls the jack and his side's first two bowls of each end. When it is his turn to bowl the jack, he must try to roll it to his skip's feet. (The skip normally stands where he wants the jack.) Then he will try to get both his woods as close as possible to the jack, preferably on the centre line of the rink.

Tip: to speed up play, fetch the mat and be ready to place it in position for the start of the next end as soon as it is clear that your side has won the end.

The second plays his side's third and fourth woods of each end. If the lead has failed, he will try to get his woods close to the jack, but he may well be asked (by his skip) to put in a positional bowl (normally behind the head in a receiving position). He will also carry the scorecard, and will keep it up to date.

Tip: don't forget your pencil — and to check the score with your opposite number at the end of each end. Try not to bowl too many short woods.

The third is the skip's lieutenant — the vice-captain of the four. He bowls his side's fifth and sixth woods of the end, and directs the head when his skip is on the mat. He is also the spokesman of the four when it comes to counting and possibly measuring the shots when each end is finished.

Tip: You may not 'claim' shots — it's up to your opposite number to concede them. But you can speed up the process politely by saying, 'I'm asking for three!' or such like. A good measure, preferably with a good set of callipers is a must.

The skip is 'in charge' of the rink, making tactical decisions, directing his players and playing his side's seventh and eighth woods every end. He

should be patient and encouraging, have a sound tactical knowledge, and be able to play 'all the shots'. He may have to draw to save, take a bowl out for a count, or kill an end by scattering woods and jacks when the position is desperate.

Tip: The lead and second are often considered to be there to 'bowl their woods and shut up', but really you would be well advised to involve them, as well as your third, in discussion. It is, after all, a team game. Be positive, and try to find something good to say about every bowl your team-mates deliver.

'Possession of the rink': when you are neither on the mat nor actually directing the head, you should keep discreetly behind the mat or behind the head, and to one side of the rink.

The lead: John Ottaway leads with machine-like accuracy. His spot-on drawing also took him to the England outdoor singles title in 1989 and to the British Isles title 1990; *The second:* Roy Cutts is an ideal second man – reliable in a crisis and enthusiastic at all times; *The third:* John Bell, a formidable international skip in his own right, has proved to be a great number three. He was a tower of strength when England struck gold at Aberdeen in 1984, and again when they won the bronze at Auckland in 1988; *The skip:* Tony Allcock, top skip in the NatWest home international series in 1990, inspires his men by his example.
(Duncan Cubitt/ Bowls International Magazine)

6 THE LAWS OF THE GAME AND ETIQUETTE

There are seventy-three Laws of the Game promulgated by the International Bowling Board (IBB), and the World Indoor Bowls Council (WIBC) have the same number. Be warned, however: although the two sets of Laws are similar, and, indeed, identical in principle, there are important differences.

The two sets of Laws are published together in one handbook, called, not surprisingly, *The Laws of the Game Governing Indoor and Outdoor Bowls.*

Every bowler should familiarize himself with the Laws, and with any domestic variations that may apply in his club or area, and even grass roots bowlers will no doubt be interested in the subtleties and niceties of some of the more complicated issues.

Here is not the place to go into fine detail, but a simplified summary of some of the more basic rules may be found below. The language has been simplified, and, for chapter and verse, readers should refer to the authentic Laws of the Game, which, as well as being available in booklet form, are printed in the annual handbooks of most national associations — certainly in the EBA Year Book.

The function of a code of Laws is to help people understand the principles of the game, and to allow them to enjoy it. Bowls is noted for its good sportsmanship, and, although the letter of the law is important, the spirit of the law is what really matters. The WIBC, in their introduction to the Laws, have included a paragraph that is well worth noting.

It should be appreciated that no code of Laws governing a game has yet achieved such perfection as to cope with every situation ... Unusual incidents not definitely provided for in the Laws frequently occur. It is well, therefore, to remember that the Laws have been framed in the belief that true sportsmanship will prevail, and that, in the absence of any express rule, common sense will find a way to complete a happy solution to a knotty problem.

There is also an unwritten code of conduct on the green which is not covered in the Laws. New bowlers, particularly, need to familiarize themselves with the etiquette of the game, because they will find that bowls, being a social game, is full of little traditions and rituals — on and off the green.

BASIC RULES EXPLAINED
STARTING A GAME — THE FIRST END

1. Skips toss for jack — winner of toss may choose to deliver the jack *or to give it away* on the first end.
2. Lead places the mat with the *back edge* 4 feet (1.22m) (front edge 6 feet [1.83m]) from the ditch and on the centre line of the rink.
3. The lead who bowls the jack also bowls the first wood of the end.

The '6-foot stick' helps to measure the distance of the mat from the ditch on the first end.
(Maurice Sims)

SUBSEQUENT ENDS

4. The winning side on each end earns the right to deliver the jack (and the first bowl) on the following end. *They may not give that right away.*

5. The mat (back edge) must still be placed at least 4 feet (1.22m) from the ditch, but may be taken up the green (allowing sufficient distance between mat and front ditch for a minimum length jack). *It must **always** be placed on the centre line of the rink.*

DEAD ENDS

6. If an end is killed, there is no penalty (except when there are domestic rules covering time-limit league play). The end must be replayed, and the jack delivered *by the winner of the previous live end.*

EXTRA ENDS

7. In the event of an extra end being required, the skips shall toss for the right to deliver the jack (or to give it away), just as if it were the first end of the match. The mat, too, must be placed as for the first end.

LIVE BOWLS

8. Any bowl is live if it comes to rest on the green *within the confines of the rink.* If any part of the bowl is on or over the rink of play, it is a live bowl. Dead bowls must be removed to the bank.

TOUCHERS

9. Any bowl which touches the jack *'in its original course'* is a toucher, and should be marked with chalk. That bowl will remain a live bowl even if it drops into the ditch during that particular end.

LIVE JACK

10. The minimum length jack (IBB Laws) is 70 feet (21.3m) from the front edge of the mat. The maximum is 6 feet (1.83m) short of the far ditch. If the lead rolls the jack short of 70 feet (21.3m), or into the ditch, *the right to deliver the jack passes to his opponent* (though he keeps the right to bowl the first

wood). If he rolls it to within 6 feet (1.83m) of the ditch, the jack will be brought out to the 6 feet (1.83m) mark.

11. *The jack must always be centred* — i.e., placed on the centre line of the rink — before the first wood is bowled. The skip normally does this in team games, and the marker in singles.

12. The jack, although it must always be placed on the centre line of the rink before the end commences, may, through impact with bowls, be moved during the course of play. It remains live if any part of it is *within the confines of the rink,* and is also in play if it drops into the ditch (again within the rink of play).

13. If, during the course of play, the jack rebounds up the rink, in the direction of the mat, it is still alive as long as the distance between the centre of the front edge of the mat and the jack is at least 61 feet (18.6m).

Touchers may now be marked without the danger of displacing the bowl. An aerosol toucha was introduced in time for the Commonwealth Games in Auckland in 1990.
(Maurice Sims)

FOOT-FAULTING

14. The Laws covering foot-faulting are intended to prevent cheating i.e. to stop a player carrying his bowl up to the head and placing it where he wants it. This law is rarely invoked. Quite simply, the *whole* of one foot should be *on (or over) the mat at the moment of delivery.*

POSSESSION OF THE RINK

15. It is perhaps worth quoting IBB Laws 50 and 51 in full. There are suspicions that, very occasionally, these Laws are flouted deliberately by unscrupulous players, so it is essential that every beginner should know exactly what is expected of him, so that he should not, through ignorance, be accused of gamesmanship.

Law 50. Possession of the Rink shall belong to the team whose bowl is being played. The players in possession of the Rink for the time being shall not be interfered with, annoyed, or have their attention distracted in any way by their opponents.

As soon as each bowl shall have come to rest, possession of the Rink shall be transferred to the other team, time being allowed for marking a 'toucher'.

Law 51. Players of each team not in the act of playing or controlling play, shall stand behind the jack and away from the head, or one yard (92 cm) behind the mat. As soon as the bowl is delivered, the skip or player directing, if in front of the jack, shall retire behind it.

HOW TO BEHAVE ON THE GREEN

In Australia, there is a charming tradition of picking up your opponent's bowl and handing it to him. Although that particular gesture is not observed very often in Britain, it is quite common to see a lead hand the jack or the mat to his opposite number.

The pace of the game of bowls allows these niceties to be observed, and it would be a shame to see them die out. Even in the most intense competitive games, it is possible to find time to lighten the tension by socializing with your opponent.

Although bowls is perhaps the most sociable of games, the need to concentrate means that conversation between the players of opposite teams must be limited, however, and, again, part of the etiquette of the game demands that you pick your moments so as not to annoy the other player.

This is covered, of course, in Laws 50 and 51, quoted in full above, but the need to behave in such a way that your opponent is not put off is also a matter of etiquette. Be careful, for example, not to move around behind the head when he is on the mat.

First, however, is the start-of-the-game ritual, when, even in a friendly roll-up, it is customary for the introductions to be made before the trial ends begin. 'Hello, George, I'm Harry,' – that sort of

The whole of one foot should be on (or above) the mat at the moment of delivery. The sequence shows: correct placement of foot; foot faulting; how an air-borne foot may be perfectly legal; a clear case of foot faulting.
(Maurice Sims)

'Have a good
game!'
(Duncan Cubitt/
International
Bowls Magazine)

thing — and, of course, 'Have a good game.'

When your opponent plays a good bowl, it costs nothing to quietly applaud or congratulate him. It is not a sign of weakness on your part, especially if next time you go to the mat you draw the shot!

Don't forget to acknowledge your own good fortune when you have a stroke of luck — and learn to take it on the chin when your opponent flukes a shot or when you have some bad luck. Luck has a tendency of evening itself out. Be patient — show your good nature and smile!

And your responsibility to your opponent does not finish when the game is over. The ritual of shaking hands is repeated, with congratulations or condolences as appropriate, and everyone retires to the clubhouse.

Most clubs either have a lounge bar of their own, or a local hostelry to which to retire after the game, and it is normal to stay with your opponent long enough to buy him a drink, not necessarily alcoholic, and take one from him in return.

New bowlers who have played other, perhaps more robust sports, are often surprised at how sociable bowls is. Keep up the traditions of our great old game, enjoy it on and off the green, and encourage others to do so.

HOW TO BEHAVE AS A CLUB MEMBER

Every club is different, so make sure **Make sure you know** you know exactly what your club ex- **exactly what your club** pects of you. What standards of dress **expects of you** do they require, on and off the green? And how do they set about picking teams?

You may be expected to put your name down on an availability list to indicate which games you are able to play. When the teams are posted, you will probably be asked to tick your name, and perhaps help out with transport.

Clubs are run, generally, by volunteers, and your services may be useful to the club — helping to tend the green, keeping the surrounds in order, serving behind the bar, assisting the secretary, serving on the committee. No one is too new to be of service, and any offers of help you can make will be most welcome.

Find out when the Annual General Meeting is, attend it, and make your contribution as an active club member. Bowls is one of the best organized of all sports — thanks partly to the overall control exerted by the national associations, but mainly through busy grass roots organization at club level.

Bowls is an extremely sociable game and it is usual to enjoy a drink with your opponent after the game.
(Maurice Sims)

7 ON-GREEN PRACTICE

Practice can take two forms − on-green and off-green. You can, in other words, rehearse your action anywhere, and learn about the game by talking about it in the club lounge.

This chapter is about what you can do on the green − not only when you go out with practice in mind, but also when you are taking part in a match.

BEING COACHED − AND COACHING YOURSELF

Your club coach, if he has an EBCS certificate, will be patient and permissive. He will allow you to develop your own style, and help you find a delivery that suits you.

At the same time, he will correct any aspects of your delivery that are likely to produce faults, and suggest exercises for you to practise on your own so that you can get 'in the groove'.

If you can't find a coach, or if he is not always available, you might find some of the following exercises useful. Some of the best practising is done solo, but a partner can often help practising is done solo, but a partner can often help. You can straighten the jack for each other, set up heads, discuss tactics and technique, and monitor each other's progress.

ANGLES AND IMPACT

Set up various positions you may have encountered yourself in a game, or maybe seen on television. Find out what happens when a bowl strikes another, by experimenting − first from a very short distance, then, when you are more adept, from the mat as in a match.

If you have played snooker or billiards before taking to bowls, the knowledge you have gained about angles and impact will be valuable. Try different angles, different speeds, and compare the results.

Experiment by setting up heads and discover what happens when one bowl strikes another.
(Maurice Sims)

DRAWING PRACTICE

Draw, draw, and draw again. That's how Hugh Duff won the world indoor title in 1988. Hugh was only twenty-four when he became world champion, and his success was the reward for hours and hours and hours of dedicated practice at the Auchinleck stadium in Ayrshire.

The man who succeeded him in 1989 was Richard Corsie, who plays a rough game at times. He fires as fast and as accurately as any British player, but he insists that he was inspired by John Summers, a Scottish lead who, according to Richard, 'could draw inside the jack!'

The 1990 champion, John Price, though he has learnt to strike, started as a specialist lead, whose drawing was a legend in Wales. He is one of the

most consistent players in the game, thanks to the years of practice he has given to the art of drawing.

Groove yourself a delivery that is dependable. That means it must be the same, time after time, not impulsive and unpredictable. It must be natural, of course, yet controlled; fluid yet contained; graceful yet economical.

When, with the help of your coach, you have sorted out a suitable delivery for you, practise it until it becomes second nature. A lot of today's top bowlers took up the game in their early teens. Their deliveries are athletic, fluid and elegant because they really are second nature: they have grown up with them.

Your delivery should, after hours of practice, become comfortable, reliable, almost automatic — so that you can concentrate not on the mechanics of technique, but on the line and length and the shot in hand.

No ideal delivery could possibly be prescribed in the pages of a book. Everyone is different and should find his or her own way of delivering a bowl, but if you want a check list to help you analyse your delivery, these are the things you could consider when you are practising. (Don't think about them during a match, whatever you do!)

Opposite: **Getting 'in the groove'. The aim of drawing practice is to deliver four identical bowls. Consistency is what you are looking for.** *(Maurice Sims)*

CHECK-POINTS

• Comfortable grip

DJB: Fingers should be approximately parallel to the running surface of the bowl. Do not let the little finger creep too far up the side of the bowl. The grip should feel comfortable and tension-free. Players with small hands or short thumbs may have to cradle the bowl.

• Even spread of fingers

DJB: Watch out particularly for the little finger. If it curls around into a high position it is likely to interfere with the smooth delivery of the bowl. Quite often it is the faulty positioning of the little finger that induces a wobble into a delivery.

The grip should be comfortable and tension free. a) In the claw grip, the thumb is held high; b) In the cradle grip, the bowl is cupped in the hand; c) Most bowlers use something in between the cradle and the claw – remember, it's comfort that counts; d) Watch for a high little finger – it can cause a wobble in your delivery; e) Spread your fingers comfortably under the bowl.
(Maurice Sims)

● Flexible wrist

DJB: Rhythm is part of the delivery process. Make sure your wrist is relaxed. If you were throwing a stone into a bucket, you would 'weigh' it in your hand, and flex your wrist before launching it through the air. The same principle applies to playing bowls.

● Position of feet on the mat

DJB: Having adopted a comfortable stance, the player should feel well balanced and tension-free. The right foot should be positioned on the mat pointing down the aiming line so that the player is facing the direction he intends to bowl.

● Length and direction of step forward

DJB: While the right foot guarantees the correct line, the stepping out with the left foot must also be

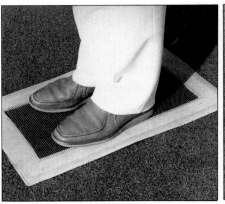 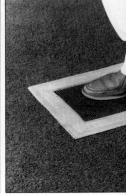

executed with care to ensure accuracy.

• Length and direction of backswing

DJB: The longer the backswing, the faster the swing – and the further the bowl is likely to travel. On heavier greens, try a longer backswing; on fast greens, try a shorter one.

• Length, direction and pace of follow-through

DJB: Likewise the follow-through. The further forward your arm is extended, the more opportunity there will have been to increase the momentum. An extended follow-through helps you to reach long jacks on heavy greens; for short jacks on fast greens, try a slower, shorter follow-through.

• Tempo and direction of forward swing

DJB: During delivery the shoulder, elbow, wrist and bowl should move smoothly down the selected

Adopt a comfortable stance. The sequence shows: the orthodox stance, with feet parallel and slightly apart; a common variation, with the body weight firmly on the right foot, and the left foot placed lightly (and temporarily) at the side; and the South African clinic style, with the left foot placed on the delivery line prior to delivery. The subsequent step forward is therefore much shorter, and direction should be automatic.
(Maurice Sims)

line. Varying the speed helps you to adjust to different speeds of green and different lengths of jack.

● Height of stance

DJB: I have found that the higher I raise my body from the crouch, the better I can cope with the heavier greens like the ones we encounter so often at the start of the outdoor season.

● Stability of stance

DJB: My own stance has its own built-in stability. Make sure that you have a solid, reliable base from which to deliver.

● Balance (before, during and after delivery)

DJB: It's all very well to have a solid stance at the *start* of your delivery, but it's also important to make sure that your movements *during* delivery do not throw you off balance. Your entire delivery must be well controlled, and rhythmic. Always go back to basic principles, and make sure all your action is well balanced.

● Positive transfer of weight from right to left foot

DJB: Your left foot does not have to be parallel to your right foot at the start of your delivery, but you must be sure to step out positively and in the right direction — precisely along the intended line — during the act of delivery.

● Position (and stillness) of head

DJB: There are many different styles of delivery — many of them unorthodox and inconsistent with what coaches might consider the ideal action. All successful players, however, have one thing in common: they keep their head perfectly still at the moment of delivery. Watch the top players, and you will confirm the truth of this theory.

● Focus for eyes (looking along the line of delivery)

DJB: To ground the bowl perfectly, the player must bend from the waist, relaxing the knees, and should keep his head down, with eyes firmly fixed on his point of aim until the bowl has left his hand.

THINGS TO DO

The best practice for drawing is simply drawing to a

jack. Place the mat, and keep it in that position. Place − or roll − the jack, and keep it there for several ends. Keep the conditions standard and stable. Cut down on variables.

Many coaching manuals recommend playing to several different lengths, all on the same end. They say it helps you to be adaptable. That comes later. It's a good advanced exercise, but, at the beginning, keep things simple. Make it easy for yourself.

You can monitor your own progress by measuring the distance of your bowls from the jack at the start of your practice session, and doing the same at the end. Consistency is what you are looking for, and you are more likely to be consistent if the practice length remains unchanged.

When you can deliver your second bowl so that it nestles up to your first, then follow with your third and fourth, you can say, 'At least there's nothing wrong with my delivery.' You have begun to group your bowls. You are getting in the groove.

Such practice needs to be continuous, and you would be well advised to stick to the same hand − say forehand one way and backhand the other. Once you have succeeded in grouping your four bowls, say within 18 inches (45 cm) of each other, you are ready for something more advanced − now you can change the length, and change your hand.

PRACTISING SHOTS

Give yourself an occasional break from the monotony of drawing practice. Try some trick shots. Set up a number of different heads and experiment with different shots, just as you did when you were learning about angles and impact (above), but this time 'for real'. That is, from the mat − a distance of at least 30 yards (27 m) away.

Try the run through shot, the trail, the split, the take-out and the drive. Don't give up until you have succeeded with each one. If you are on your own, take two or three sets of bowls on to the rink, so that you can have more attempts before you have to walk to the head.

If you miss, it's sometimes a good discipline to force yourself to walk up the rink to retrieve your bowl and repeat the attempt. Try to build the atmosphere of a real match in your mind, creating the 'pressure' of a crisis situation or a world championship final.

It's rather like the boy playing cricket who imagines he's at Lord's, or playing soccer who believes he's scoring a goal at Wembley. But that's legitimate role-play, and anything that stimulates what top coaches call purposeful practice has got to be good.

Ian Schuback, the top Australian, who believes in practice, practice and more practice, says he dramatizes the situations in his mind in exactly this way. He hates the traditional roll-up, where you play a 'proper' game, and would rather not practise at all if that was all that was on offer.

MATCH PRACTICE

'Practising' during a game can exercise your mind or your body — preferably both. And it can involve learning more about tactics as well as technique. However long you have been playing bowls, you can be sure there is always something new to learn.

And, however much practice you have put in with the coach or on your own, there is nothing quite like testing out your action and technique 'in active service'. The more you play in matches, the more you will develop your game.

It is noticeable, for example, even at the top level, that those players who make their first visit to the portable rink to make their début in a televised event, find it difficult to come to terms with the strange conditions — the cameras, the lights, the single-rink, the theatrical atmosphere, and the wooden floor.

Those who have been there before are far more at home and likely to do well. Success breeds success. That is what experience is all about. Whether you realize it or not, you are learning all the time. And the more you play, the more you learn.

TRIAL ENDS

The first thing to learn − before the game actually starts − is how the green is behaving. That is what the trial ends are for. Even before you step on the green, your powers of observation will tell you if the grass has been cut, or if the covering is patchy.

Look out for signs that one hand may be faster than the other. Perhaps one side of the rink has less grass, perhaps it is a lighter colour than the other side of the rink, or perhaps the grass appears to have been rolled flatter on one side than the other.

In the last case, it's quite possible, if you are starting an evening game, that the rink was played on during the afternoon − in which case, the players in that game may have concentrated their efforts on one hand − maybe because they found the other one a bit tricky.

In any case, if the rink has been played on earlier in the day, it will probably have the 'tracking' marks of the previous session's woods, giving a clue as to the nature of the two hands, or sides of the rink. Often one will be wider than the other − a 'swinger', and a 'straight' hand.

If there are no tracks to guide you, it is a useful tip to aim at the rink boundary peg. On a true and average British green, that's the amount of swing you can expect. Watch your first trial bowl all the way up the rink, observing how it swings. Does it check, straighten, or go against the bias? Or does it bend more than you expected, finishing narrow?

Whatever it does, it is a simple and straightforward matter of adjusting with your next delivery. If you are playing four woods on the trial ends (as you are entitled to in singles and pairs) try to correct with your very next bowl. But, don't be so preoccupied with testing the hand that you neglect the other hand. Always try both sides of the rink on the trial ends.

The next thing to assess is the pace of the green. If the grass looks lush, dark green, or wet, you can be fairly sure that you will need to heave the bowl up the green. If it is cut short, burnt yellow or brown, it could be free, and very little impetus will be required.

Sometimes, particularly indoors, the jack does not seem to travel at the same pace as the woods. If the underlay is thick and soft, but the top surface hard, you will find that the jack will fly, and you may lose it in the ditch. Bowls, because they are heavier, will sink through the top surface and are likely to be slowed down by the thick underlay.

The trial ends will tell you this. Be on the look-out for such features. Indeed, the track of the jack, unbiased as it is, may well give you a clue as to the levels of the rink. Watch its course down the rink. Does it waver? Does it finish its journey by swinging one way? If so, you'll be able to guess which is the swinging hand.

TACTICS

Playing in a match is a great way of learning about tactics. Watch the skip, listen to what he says, and try to work out why he is playing the shot he has chosen. Try, also, to work out what other options he may have had. And what you would have done in the same circumstances.

If you are playing lead or second, you had better not ask questions during the match, or make any comment unless you are asked, but a good skip will never be afraid to be quizzed afterwards − in the clubhouse − about his choice of tactics.

To be a good tactician involves reading a head, and you can do that at any time. These are the sorts of questions to ask yourself before deciding what shot to play:

WHEN WE HOLD THE SHOT
- Have we any other bowls in the head?
- Have we got a back bowl?
- Is it dangerous to try to draw another?
- Could we easily give it away?
- Is there a danger of widening the head?
- Is it already vulnerable?
- Could our shot do with tidying up?

- Do we really need another shot?
- Should we try to protect our shot with a blocker?
- What is our opponent likely to play?
- What does our opponent not want us to do?

WHEN THE SHOT IS AGAINST US

- How many shots do they hold?
- Have we got anything close?
- Do we need a good second?
- What could go wrong if we play weight?
- Could we be any worse off?
- What is the safest shot to play?
- What is the safest weight to play it with?
- Where is the jack going to go?
- Who has the back bowls?
- Who has the bowls in the best receiving position?
- If we take one of our woods out, can our opponent make a count?
- If we get the shot, will the opponent be tempted to fire?
- Is it better to concede one than risk a disaster?

8 OFF-GREEN ACTIVITY

If you have been bitten by the bowls bug, you'll want to get on the green as often as possible — to practise or play. But it is not always possible to find a rink available.

Outdoors, during the summer, greens are usually full in the evenings. If there isn't a club match on, the county championships are likely to be in full swing. There are club fixtures in the afternoons, too, but not every day, and you may well be able to book a rink for some coaching or practice.

Indoors, in the winter months, rinks are normally fully booked up, because indoor clubs are run on business lines and must pay for themselves. Competitive leagues are therefore arranged, morning, afternoon and evening, and a casual roll-up, or a practice session is difficult if not impossible to fit in.

All is not lost. Very keen beginners can sometimes arrange to creep into the indoor club, and have a practice session before the leagues start. Usually they are scheduled to begin at 10 a.m. or 10.30 a.m. so, if you are an early bird, you may be lucky.

PRACTISING AT HOME

In any case, you don't need a full sized green to practise some of the basic essentials of your delivery. You can rehearse your stance and action at home, with or without a wood in your hand.

Some coaches believe that to go through your delivery without a bowl is artificial, and therefore counter-productive. But, in terms of loosening your

Practise at home. Put a cushion up against the wall and roll the wood towards it.
(Maurice Sims)

Bending your knees helps to achieve a smooth, rhythmic delivery.
(Maurice Sims)

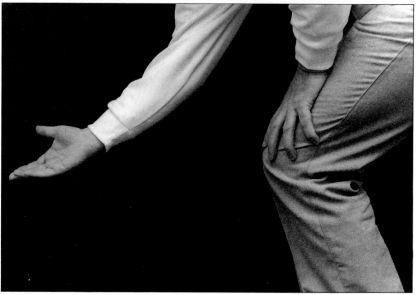

leg and back muscles, and getting them used to a new movement, going through your action in your lounge − or anywhere − is to be recommended.

Golfers do it with their swing. They can often be seen, in a loose moment, having a go at an imaginary ball. And they don't seem the slightest bit self-conscious about it. Imagine the style you would like to have, and try to groove it − in the privacy of your own home.

It is obviously preferable to simulate actual playing conditions as far as possible, so a wood in your hand is a good idea. Put a cushion up against the wall, and roll the wood towards it. The important thing is to get your delivery consistent. Don't worry about where the bowl is going − but try not to miss the cushion!

WATCHING THE BEST

Take every opportunity you have to watch the best bowlers in action. If there is an important cup match at your club, go along and watch. If it is a close match, you will find it exciting, but don't allow the excitement to cloud your ability to learn.

Deliveries are so different, varying from person to person, that it is possible to forget that all good bowlers have a lot in common. Their consistency depends on factors that You can observe and analyse for yourself — if you take the trouble to stop and look.

Watch the best bowlers closely – observe and analyse

Watch them closely − the accepted top-notchers in your own club and the visiting stars, and analyse how they stand on the mat, how they step forward, where they are looking at the moment of delivery, and how they ground the bowl. Notice how, whatever their personal idiosyncrasies, their heads are still at the moment the bowl leaves their hands.

They may have an unorthodox stance. It is surprising, in fact, how few top players stand on the mat with their feet parallel. Most coaches recommend this, but it is clearly not necessary. But, however they stand, nearly all will step out with their left foot, and plant it firmly and accurately in the direction they intend to launch the bowl.

Some bowlers look for their line first, then turn their attention to the jack, and will be staring straight up the green as they deliver. Some will be looking at the ground a few metres in front of them. A few may even be looking at their feet. It is much more usual, though, for the successful player to be looking along the line of his intended delivery.

Most agree that the first thing to do is to assess the distance of the jack from the mat by looking at the jack. Then, carrying the information that governs weight, they do not look at the jack again, preferring to concentrate on the line.

Not every good bowler has a perfect delivery. But, if he doesn't, he probably wishes he did. As you get older, it is inevitable that your grounding of the bowl is less smooth than it was in your youth. But it is worth striving for perfection.

If you wobble your bowl, or bump it, you can get away with it if the wobble or bump is consistent. But it is better to tackle the problem, which can often be overcome by getting lower to the ground. Try stooping towards the line. Try bending your knees. Try to brush the turf — or carpet — with your fingers as you go through with your delivery.

This is a problem that coaches often encounter, and a good coach can certainly help to eradicate any faults. In general, the better bowlers are the ones with the sweetest deliveries. But, remember, it is better to have a suspect delivery and finish on the jack, than to have the most elegant style in the world and finish 2 yards away!

TELEVISION

As with most sports, television gives us the close-ups, the angled shots and replays that can help us analyse actions and styles, and even see, in slow motion, what happens, for example, when someone fires.

DJB

I was told that Terry Sullivan re-designed his delivery in 1984, basing his new style on a mixture of several bowlers' deliveries he had studied on television. Apparently, I was one of the bowlers he had studied, and, although our styles do not appear to have much in common, there are aspects of his pendulum swing that he copied from mine.

I'm not claiming the credit for his success, but it is interesting that, after putting so much study into the subject, and altering his own technique, he won the UK singles in November 1984, and the world indoor singles championship in February 1985.

DRJ

I was never a great spectator of bowls before I became part of the BBC's commentary team. Being a commentator does force you to watch what is happening, and to do so with a fresh, analytical approach.

My standard of play may not have improved as a result, but I feel I know much more about the game now than I did when I was a regular England player. I am not playing as much as I used to — there just isn't time — but I am enjoying the game at least as much now from what I call 'the best seat in the house' as I was when I was on the green.

If you have a video recorder, try recording a game on TV, and play it back, using the freeze frame and slow motion facilities. Stop the action after every bowl, and, if you are watching with a friend, discuss the possibilities for the next shot. Slow down the action of the player you admire, and think about what he does that you don't! You will learn a surprising amount about technique, and tactics.

BOOKS

There are now a lot of books available to help you learn more about bowls. At last bowls is catching up with other sports. Golf and cricket have a rich heritage of literature supporting them. There is no reason why bowls shouldn't appeal to the well-read

in exactly the same way.

Here are a few of the books that have been published in the last few years:

- *Bowl with Bryant* by David Bryant (Collins Willow 1984)
- *Bryant on Bowls* by David Bryant (Pelham Books Ltd 1985)
- *Improve your Bowls* by Tony Allcock (Collins 1987)
- *End to End: Year in Bowls* by Tony Allcock (Heinemann 1989)
- *Bowls Skills — A step by step guide* by Tony Allcock (Hamlyn 1988)
- *Bowls: The Records* by Patrick Sullivan (Guinness 1986)
- *Bowls Year Book* by Donald Newby (Pan Books/

Read, learn and inwardly digest – there are plenty of bowls books available these days.
(Maurice Sims)

Daily Telegraph)
- *The New BBC Book of Bowls* by Keith Phillips (BBC 1990)
- *The Story of Bowls: From Drake to Bryant* Ed. Phil Pilley (Stanley Paul 1987)
- *What a Load o' Bowls: I'm all right Jack* by Don East (Stanley Paul 1987)

Most of them are instructional or informative volumes, but some are merely entertaining, and it is an encouraging sign that bowls is beginning to generate publications containing anecdotes, and funny stories about the game.

Tony Allcock's *End to End* for example, is an interesting account of his first year as a professional bowler, while Don East's *What a Load o' Bowls* is a humorous but perceptive account of a beginner's struggles to master the game.

Donald Newby, the bowls correspondent of the *Daily Telegraph,* edits an annual Year Book, which seems to be set to become the *Wisden* of bowls, while Phil Pilley's *The Story of Bowls* is an anthology of bowls writing from Shakespeare to the *Sun.*

MAGAZINES

There are three bowls magazines currently available in the United Kingdom. *Scots Bowler* concerns itself only with what is happening north of the border, while *World Bowls* and *Bowls International* compete for the international market.

Bowls International is the more dazzling publication, with modern design and good photography, while *World Bowls* more soberly reflects the solid, traditional, grass roots aspects of the game.
- *Scots Bowler,* 32 Candleriggs, Alloa, Clackmannanshire, FK10 1EA
- *World Bowls,* PO Box 17, East Horsley, Surrey, KT24 5JU
- *Bowls International,* PO Box 100, Stamford, Lincs, PE9 2JR

VIDEOS

The Australians were into coaching before the English Bowls Coaching Scheme was formed in 1980, and produced a coaching film called *In the Groove* many years ago. It is now available on video, as is a British-made video called *Masterclass*. A set of four videos entitled *Tony Allcock's Art of Bowls* is also available, featuring Tony's own step-by-step guide to winning play. These are produced by Pedigree Films and distributed by Clean River Productions, Unit B11, Trinity Business Centre, 305 Rotherhithe Street, London SE16 1EY. (071) 231 6137.

For coaches in England, the EBCS produces training videos, giving examples of modern coaching methods, but, so far at least, they have been made exclusively for the coach — not the beginner himself. Tapes so far produced include: *Coaching a Beginner; Coaching Tips; Freezing Heads.*

Enquiries about the EBCS coaching tapes should be made to the Video Producer, EBCS, or the National Director of Coaching, EBCS (see Chapter 12 for addresses).

9 A WORLD OF OPPORTUNITY

Bowls is the most open of all sports. There are virtually no privileges to set the champion apart from the novice. Whatever your motives for taking up the game, make the most of any opportunities you will have to play with and against the top players in your club and your locality. And there is nothing to stop you, too, getting to the top.

There are no other sports where the complete novice can turn up at his club and find he's taking part in the same game as the club champion – and on equal terms! A new club member at Clevedon, Tommy Banner, an entertainer with the West Country pop-group, The Wurzels, was attracted to the game when he took part in a Pro/Celebrity bowls event – and soon found himself partnered regularly on Thursday evenings by Jimmy Hobday, the 1980 world triples champion.

A complete novice can find he's taking part in the same game as the club champion, and on equal terms

'All the guys are so nice and friendly,' says Tommy, 'I think bowls is a great game, and bowlers among the nicest people I've met. There is no side to them at all. Here am I, a complete and utter novice – and they accept me on the green as an equal. It's marvellous!'

You can, like Tommy, soon become absorbed into the game. As a beginner, you are putting your foot on the bottom rung of the ladder. The ladder is continuous, and the sky's the limit. Every level of bowls has its own flavour and excitement, and, basically, every stage of your bowls career involves the same striving for perfection.

And, whenever you bowl what we call a dead-length toucher, remember that no-one can ever do any better than that – even in the final of the world championship. You may not have great ambitions to climb the ladder – fair enough. But you might like to share the experience of the authors, who have enjoyed the satisfaction of watching and playing at every level of the game. Come with us, up the ladder . . . we'll tell you what to expect.

ROLL-UPS

The first thing you should do when you join a club is to contact the club coach, and get a rough-and-ready delivery sorted out so that you can fairly consistently get a bowl rolling away in more or less the right direction.

Then get in as much practice as you can, either on your own or with some friends. Casual roll-ups are helpful to groove in an action, as long as you are not too casual. Use them positively, and think about what you are doing – but don't get tense. Relax, and enjoy yourself – but analyse what is happening to your bowl as it leaves your hand and reacts to the playing surface.

FRIENDLY GAMES

As soon as you can, put your name down on the club availability list for a friendly game against another club. You may not be picked first time, but don't be shy. Above all don't take the attitude, 'I'm not good enough yet. I'd let the side down. I think I'll wait until I've attained a higher degree of performance.' Such modesty is attractive, and such reticence understandable – but the quickest way for you to make progress is to 'have a go' in a 'proper match'. No-one will be expecting miracles, but you will find you will be welcomed into the club side with a warm handshake – and you will be surprised what a contribution you will be able to make.

As for your standard of play, just look at the form of some of your team-mates who have been playing for years, and you will surely be encouraged. It's nice to win, and satisfying to play well, but never was the old adage more true, it's not the winning, but the taking part that counts.

You will find that you will be selected as lead or second at first, so you should practise drawing to the jack, ignoring the temptation to play heavy shots in your practice sessions. If you play at lead, remember the importance of casting the jack, and practise this aspect of the game. If you play second, remember you'll be keeping the scorecard, so arm youself with a pencil.

Until you are picked to play in a friendly match, you will have been restricted to playing on your own club's green. If you are chosen for an away fixture, that's when your experience will be increased, and you will grow as a bowler.

Adapting to new conditions is what bowls is all about, and playing well at home simply is not enough. Away greens may be faster or heavier, smooth as silk or badly kept, level or tricky, and you will have to adjust your swing, and perhaps take an entirely different sort of line to the jack. Try not to complain — even though your club-mates may do so. Getting to grips with a variety of conditions is part of the challenge of the game, and is all part of the fun.

Friendly games are social — and sociable — occasions. A meal will usually be provided, and there will be speeches from the captains. Bowls would not be bowls without them. The ritual of the game annoys some, but there is undoubtedly a charm to it all, and you would be wise to endure the speeches patiently.

You will doubtless be asked to contribute to the cost of the meal when playing at home, and to the cost of transport and green fees when playing away. If you have a car, you may be asked to help out with transport, and if you do, make sure you limit your intake of alcohol.

After-match socializing is one of the most attractive features of bowls. You will be expected to stay around at least long enough to buy your opponent a drink, and to take one off him. This will give you time to get to know him better — and to indulge, no doubt, in an off-the-cuff post-mortem of the match, the result of which, your captain will have reminded you, was not important!

CLUB MATCHES — LEAGUE AND CUP FIXTURES

Most clubs take part in 'serious' matches as well as the good old bread-and-butter friendlies. Some join a local league, where competition is fierce, and winning appears to be everything. There is also an inter-club knockout competition in most counties where clubs are invited to play for a coveted trophy.

Clevedon, for example, enters the Clevedon & District league, which involves eight clubs from an area around the town stretching from Portishead to

Club matches are the bread and butter of bowls. This one is being played at the authors' club at Clevedon.
(Maurice Sims)

Congresbury. The Somerset club championship is for the Turnbull Cup, and involves all 70 clubs in the county, playing first on a regional basis then on an open knockout system from the quarter finals onwards.

Good advice to the new bowler: don't leave it too long before you make yourself available for these more competitive games. Don't be modest. The decision of whether you are ready for league or cup games should be left to the selectors – not yourself! Exposure to the demands of competitive play will increase your experience, and teach you more about the game.

If you are not selected for these big matches, turn up and support your team. Watch the attitude of your club's skips to these games, and learn from the tactics and skills of visiting players. Absorb the atmosphere of the occasion, so that you will be ready when your turn comes.

COUNTY COMPETITIONS

Selection is always a bone of contention, and usually there are only sixteen places available in the club's first team. There is one way, however, that any bowler can side-step the selection process and make progress in the competitive world of bowls without waiting to get the nod from his (or her) club selectors.

As soon as possible, every bowler, whether competitively minded or not, should enter the county or national championships. These are 'open' championships – in England at any rate – and democratically allow every bowler a crack at the national titles in singles, pairs, triples and fours.

There is no seeding in bowls. Even last year's national champion has to enter the championship at club level the following season, although the way it works is slightly different indoors and outdoors.

In both, you enter from your club, and are restricted in your choice of partners to members of that club. But, while outdoors the county competitions are used as a qualifying process for the national finals held annually at Worthing, your indoor entry takes you direct into the national championships — although, again, the early stages are played off on a regional basis.

No experience is necessary before you can enter these championships, but they are a wonderful way of gaining experience. The magic of bowls is that everyone has an equal chance. As a good friend of the authors, Chris Ward, twice EBA singles champion, once said, 'I've had a look in his bag, and he's only got four woods — just the same as me!'

Have a go at the singles, and never be afraid of coming up against one of the top stars: the worst you can do is to lose, and you will learn a lot in the process. And, bowls being what it is, you never know — remember, he'll only be allowed four woods!

PLAYING FOR YOUR COUNTY

English counties play friendly fixtures against other counties, normally midweek, when they pick a team from players who are available. This usually means that the counties are not exactly at full strength, but

DRJ and DJB (*far right*) playing for Somerset against Cumbria in 1983. *(Duncan Cubitt/ Bowls International Magazine)*

there is still a feeling of pride at being selected, and being entitled to wear one's county badge — normally awarded after three (or perhaps five) games at county level.

In England, the thirty-five counties affiliated to the EBA contest the inter-county team championship for the Middleton Cup, and indoors a growing number of fully fledged counties fight it out for the Liberty Trophy every winter. There is a similar contrast between county friendlies and Middleton or Liberty matches as there is at club level between club friendlies and league or cup matches.

For both of the authors, the first time they were selected for Somerset's Middleton Cup team was a great moment. DJB recalls the thrill of playing second to Winscombe's England player, Ronnie Weeks, in 1952, while DRJ, who had already played for Carmarthenshire and the Welsh Under 35 side before moving into Somerset, remembers the nerves he felt when he made his Somerset début at Melcombe Regis in 1965.

Just as, at club level, every bowler is influenced first by the top players in his own club, then by the stars of visiting clubs, so the contact with great bowlers of other counties has an impact on the development of the rising player at county level. DJB certainly remembers those early Middleton Cup matches, and recognizes how they had a formative effect on his bowling career.

DJB

Playing against the giants of the game was a chance to marvel at their skills but also to pick up points. I could hardly believe I was on the same green as these players, whose names were so well known to me . . . Fred Horn, Harold Shapland and Harold Webber of Devon; Maurice Ferris of Cornwall; and, of course, the great Percy Baker of Dorset, who won the EBA singles four times.

Middleton Cup bowls was the tops, the pinnacle, and I played in all three games in our south west area that first season, and, though I was nervous, I

seem to remember playing very well in all three. I was on the ladder, and, at the time, it felt as if I had already reached the top. But, looking back, it was all part of the learning experience.

Not every reader of this book will be privileged to climb this far, but the opportunity of learning from better players, wherever and whenever they appear, is open to all. It may not be that you can − or even should − copy what the good bowler is doing, but there is always something to be learnt.

Perhaps it is a matter of temperament, or attitude. Perhaps it is a tactical or strategic ploy. Perhaps it is a question of determination, single-mindedness or the power of concentration. There is, for example, always an air of confidence about the class player, giving spectators − and opponents − the impression that, come what may, he believes he's going to win.

Observe him with the same eagerness that I observed the Horns and Bakers of my youth, and analyse what he's got that others haven't.

The excitement of the national championships. Terry Heppell and Martyn Sekjer lead the charge to the EBA fours title, between Blackheath and Greenwich, in 1989.
(Duncan Cubitt/ Bowls International Magazine)

PLAYING FOR YOUR COUNTRY

Climbing one rung further up the ladder, it is every Middleton Cup bowler's ambition to be nominated by his county for an England trial. That honour came to DJB in 1958, to DRJ in 1967. Both were rewards for success in the national championships, demonstrating how national titles are used as a means of measuring success.

The home outdoor international series is played between teams from England, Ireland, Scotland and Wales, each country putting six rinks of four players on the green. (For some reason, before 1990, national teams comprised only five rinks!) The festival lasts for three days, the time it takes to complete a round robin, and the atmosphere is electric. There are, of course, forty-eight players on the green at a time, all agog with excitement.

Mark Anstey becomes airborne as he gets one in for Wales in the home international series at Llanelli against Scotland, in 1987.
(Duncan Cubitt/ Bowls International Magazine)

DJB

I had skipped a Clevedon rink, including my father, Reg, and the Harris father and son combination, to

the English fours title in 1957, and was selected to play three in the trial. I was lucky enough to be chosen as three to Worthing's talented skip, John Scadgell, with the great Norman King at lead and Surrey's Ken Coulson at two.

The international series, even then, was entirely different from anything I had ever experienced in my bowling career. Every upwardly mobile bowler will, I am sure, experience this ladder effect. As you progress up the ladder, every rung brings something new, something which, I suppose, tests anew the player's ability to cope at that level.

The bowling itself is not very different. You still have to get as close as you can to the jack — and loose heads do occur, just as they do at club level! But the pressures are different. Just as there is a marked contrast between friendlies and cup matches at club level, there is the world of difference between Middleton Cup games and international play.

For one thing, the noise level at the internationals is deafening. It is the ultimate test . . . playing for your country . . . England expects . . . . every eye is watching . . . the pressure is enormous. But it is also the most thrilling and fulfilling experience . . . the camaraderie . . . the team-work . . . the elation of a good shot . . . you feel 10 feet tall.

When things are going well, I can't think of anything finer. But when things are going badly, it can be very lonely out there. At the end of the day, what the selectors — and the supporters — are looking for is consistency and reliability under pressure. Just like the selectors and supporters at club level!

DRJ

For me, selection for an England trial in 1967 — and eventually for England in 1970 — was something I had to come to terms with, being a proper Welshman through and through. However, although I had learnt to 'despise' those white jerseys at Cardiff Arms Park, it didn't take me long to realize what an honour it was to be chosen to play for England — and I have never had any difficulty in being English on the bowling green!

Some of my compatriots from South Wales, and some Scots as well, have expressed surprise that I could forsake the nation of my birth and play for my adopted country. But others have taken the same decision: before me there was Ralph Lewis, a Sussex schoolmaster, and a brilliant left-hander, and now there's Wynne Richards, who reached two Welsh finals before exchanging Troedyrhiw for Twickenham.

My first international appearance was in Glasgow in 1970, when, playing second to DJB, I marvelled at meeting the legendary Jock McAtee face to face. The sense of occasion generated at the international series has given me as many memories of the pomp and ceremony, the packed crowds, and the warmth and friendliness of the competitors from the four countries, as I have of what happened on the green.

If you haven't been to an international series, either as a player or a spectator, your bowls education is incomplete. If you get the chance, take it. The noise and colour, the excitement, the fellowship and rivalry between the players and supporters of England, Ireland, Scotland and Wales, makes the carnival unique.

The Scots were, for me, the intense nation, the professional bowlers. When I started, they had team-work taped. Their dogged, dour approach was lightened and animated, however, by an intimidating, effervescent enthusiasm, as they pranced after their bowls and rejoiced at their success. Jubilant Scots congratulated each other on every bowl, wherever it finished, shaking hands, slapping backs, and doing a jig. They were irresistible.

The Welsh had their individual characters, too, but they seemed to lack the integrated team spirit of the Scots. My initiation to international bowls came at a time when the Barry foursome were at their peak — Russell Evans, Jim Morgan, Ron Thomas and Gareth Humphries, who won the British fours title indoors and out. Then there was that chirpy little character, Jimmy John, with his self-congratulatory phrase, 'Every egg a bird!'

The Irish had characters aplenty: Percy Watson, Pat McGuirk, Gerry Crossey, Jimmy Donnelly, Roy Fulton and Syd Thompson, to name but a few. They were followed by the likes of Brendan McBrien, Stan Espie and Sammy Allen, and there will be no shortage of excitement in future years with Jim Baker, David Corkill and Michael Dunlop in the team. Brilliant players, and good talkers too. One of these days they'll get their act together on the green.

There are no apologies for these reminiscences, because, for both the authors, there will always be something special about the international series. Talk of financial restraints has prompted proposals to make the series a much more limited affair, with perhaps five or ten players per side, and with an emphasis on singles. Although this would be an interesting competition, similar to the test series played between New Zealand and Australia, a lot would be lost if the present system was discarded.

COMMONWEALTH GAMES

The Commonwealth Games is a grand showpiece for bowls — proud to be one of the original sports when the Empire Games was first held in 1930. Since then, bowls has missed out only once — in 1966, when the Games visited Jamaica, where there are, sadly, no bowling greens.

The Games now offers equal opportunities for men and women, with championships for singles, pairs and fours for both sexes. Most countries, therefore, enter teams of fourteen players, seven men and seven women, with a manager and manageress who double as reserves for their national teams.

When the number of competing countries made it possible, a complete round robin was played to decide the winner — the man or woman who topped the final league table. Entries in 1990 made it necessary, for the first time, to split the entries into two groups, with a gold medal play-off between the winners of the two sections, and a play-off for bronze between the two runners up.

DJB

I have long and happy associations with the Friendly Games, as the Commonwealth Games are often called. I regard the Games as a chance for bowls to hold its head up among the other sports, and I have found an increasing respect for our game from the devotees of the other disciplines as the years have rolled on.

Perhaps it is because the athletes have watched bowls on television, but there was certainly a lot more awareness shown by the competitors in the Games Village at Auckland than I have ever experienced before. We used to be the Cinderella sport of the Games, but I'm pleased to say that there was tremendous interest in our activities in 1990.

My first involvement in the Games came in 1962, when I took part in the singles and pairs – in those days a team of four would compete as a rink, then split up to play singles and pairs, with one team

Grant Knox and George Adrain came through the Commonwealth Games unbeaten and struck gold in the pairs at Balgreen, Edinburgh, in 1986.
(Duncan Cubitt/ Bowls International Magazine)

member resting. In those unenlightened days, women were not given the chance to compete at all.

Standing on the podium for the medal ceremony at Perth was a new experience for me, and it was a thrill that will live with me for ever. The culmination of so much hard preparation, the discipline of coming to terms with the fast Australian greens, and the grind of having to play against every one of the other competitors in a gruelling round robin. It was all worth while. I was euphoric, and the sense of relief was tremendous.

The best thing of all, I believe, was the comradeship, not only within the English team, but among all the competitors from all over the world. And, of course, the way in which the bowls events have become more popular is of great satisfaction to me. At Perth, there were thirteen countries taking part in the bowls, but at Auckland — twenty-eight years later — there were nineteen.

It's wonderful to see how the game has spread among the so-called emerging nations, who add so much to the Games: Geua Tau's win for Papua New Guinea in the women's singles will do great things for bowls all over the world, and it is good to see Cook Islands, Norfolk Island, and India taking part.

DRJ

DJB's love affair with the Commonwealth Games started in 1962, and is still going strong. But he has left the most remarkable story untold: the extent of his own domination of the men's singles, and his incredible record, which he came so close to extending in 1990 — and which he might well earn another crack at in Victoria in 1994.

DJB won the singles gold medal in Perth (1962), Edinburgh (1970), Christchurch (1974) and Edmonton (1978). Out of contention in 1982 and 1986 because the bowls administrators deemed him to be a professional, he missed out on two chances to create the outstanding record of having won five gold medals at the same event in five separate Games.

In Auckland in 1990, he came so close to that coveted record, needing only two more shots against the eventual champion, Rob Parrella to qualify for the gold medal play-off. Requiring 16, he had to settle for 14, and the chance of meeting Hong Kong's twenty-year-old sensation, Mark McMahon, in what would have been a memorable final, had gone.

He can console himself, however, that he still shares the record of four golds from four Games with his old weightlifting friend, ex-Bristolian, Precious McKenzie, whose association with the Commonwealth Games is as romantic as his own.

Over the years, DJB has played sixty-two singles matches in five Commonwealth Games, winning

fifty-five — a record that will surely never be matched. And he's not finished yet! He still harbours hopes of going for gold again at Victoria in 1994.

WORLD CHAMPIONSHIPS

Although the history of bowls makes it a predominantly Commonwealth sport, the world outdoor championships admit a number of countries outside 'the family of the old Empire'. Of these, the USA is the strongest, but world bowls is enriched by the participation of Argentina, Israel and Japan. From a playing point of view, the world championships suffer by the continued disqualification of South Africa.

'Hats off to England!' – (l-r) John Bell, Tony Allcock, Julian Haines, George Turley and DJB won the Leonard Trophy at World Bowls (Aberdeen) in 1984. With John Ottaway replacing Turley and Wynne Richards replacing Haines, England retained the team title at Auckland in 1988.
(Duncan Cubitt/ Bowls International Magazine)

The first **World Bowls** was held in 1966, prompted no doubt by the thought that, with no bowls in Jamaica, there would otherwise be a spell of eight years without a major international competition. It was such a rip-roaring success that it was introduced on a regular basis, once every four years, in between Commonwealth Games.

Countries affiliated to the IBB are entitled to enter teams of five players, who start the event as a triple and pair, regrouping in the second half of the championships to contest singles and fours. Championships have so far been held at Kyeemagh, Sydney (1966), Worthing (1972), Johannesburg (1976), Frankston, Melbourne (1980), Aberdeen (1984) and Henderson, Auckland (1988).

The International Women's Bowling Board (IWBB) have followed the pattern set by the men, and have held their championships at Sydney (1969), Wellington (1973), Worthing (1977), Toronto (1981), Melbourne (1985) and Auckland (1988).

DJB

Though some of my most pleasant memories derive from Commonwealth Games, it is the world championships that carry the most prestige. There is, after all, something special about being able to describe yourself as the World Champion, and, for bowlers, the world championships have to be regarded as the major event.

One thing I regret very much about the world championships is the decision to abandon the round robin − although the reasons for the decision are unimpeachable. With possibly thirty countries putting in for the next World Bowls, it would be impracticable to schedule everyone to play everyone else.

From a player's point of view, however, a round robin is the only totally satisfactory way of determining the true champion. Nevertheless, I accept that some sort of grouping is necessary, because, with any luck, there are going to be even more entries in future, now that there are signs that bowls is spreading into Europe.

Pressures to limit the entries to the so-called strongest countries, should, in my view, be resisted, as every one of the countries sending competitors to World Bowls adds something special to the flavour of the event. And some of the smaller countries are capable of springing a surprise or two. For that reason, I would never stop them entering the world championships.

Hong Kong, with fewer than 800 male bowlers, have long been a force in the bowling world, while Papua New Guinea are now regarded as a real threat to the established countries. In 1988, at Henderson, Guernsey's Mike Nicolle made his presence felt when he beat Aussie, Kenny Williams, and denied him a place in the final. And Argentina's Jose Riveros pulled off a fine win over Willie Wood.

DRJ

What DJB has omitted to mention is his own record in World Bowls. He won the singles at the inaugural event in 1966, but turned in a disappointing performance at Worthing in 1972. The South Africans monopolized the championships at Johannesburg in 1976, but DJB came back strongly in 1980, winning not only the singles but the triples as well.

At Aberdeen in 1984, when, for the first time, the round robin games were played in two groups, he narrowly missed a place in the singles final, but grabbed the bronze medal and helped Tony Allcock to the pairs silver. Then, in Auckland in 1988, he was back in business again with a fairy-tale win over Willie Wood in the singles final — and took the silver medal again with Tony in the pairs.

I was there when DJB played the shot of a lifetime to beat Willie in that 1988 final in front of a crowd of several thousand. He had come back from 21-12 to tie the scores, 22-all, when the heavens opened and flooded the greens. Over an hour later, they returned to the rink for what amounted to a game of three-up.

Willie played four perfect bowls, but it was DJB

who somehow scored the three shots, firing all of Willie's woods off the rink before the rains came down again. DJB's final delivery struck Willie's shot and cannoned it on to his next nearest, whereupon DJB's cannonball, following through, miraculously struck the shot bowl for the second time and removed it from the rink.

The shot had a large element of luck, and provoked much comment, most of it sympathetic to Willie: but no-one could deny that DJB had played the shot perfectly under pressure. It's surely part of the magic of the man that he seems so often to conjure his own luck − and rescues himself from seemingly impossible situations.

TELEVISED BOWLS

The **world indoor championships** are an entirely different kind of competition, whose development has been linked very much with sponsorship and television coverage. Some may say that makes the championship, like indoor bowls itself, an artificial and contrived creation. But there is no doubt that it produces some of the finest bowling ever witnessed − and that it is one of the most difficult competitions to win.

Sponsored since 1979 by Embassy, the world indoor singles was conceived in Scotland, and staged for ten years at the famous Coatbridge club near Glasgow. The claustrophobic Coatbridge cockpit became the home of indoor bowls, but, in 1988, the event was moved to Alexandra Palace, which offered more in the way of backstage facilities for players and officials, and thence to the Preston Guild Hall, which has staged so many snooker and bowls championships.

British players have always dominated the event, mainly because indoor bowls is stronger in Britain than anywhere else in the world. At first, there were a handful of invited players from the UK, joined by two or three overseas hopefuls, and there were charges that it was not a real world championship. Now there is a complicated qualification process, allowing more players to take part, and ensuring they are there on merit. The overseas stars are given more time to acclimatize to the conditions before they take to the portable rink, and some of them, too, have to win their way into the event through a qualifying tournament in their home country.

Some of the overseas players are now among the top challengers, and show an increasingly professional attitude to their visit to the United Kingdom. The prize money − £20,000 first prize in 1990 − helps, no doubt, to concentrate the mind, and, in 1987, Ian Schuback and Jim Yates became the first overseas players to win a major indoor event in the UK when they walked off with the Midland Bank world pairs title.

DJB

There is little to choose between the CIS UK indoor singles championship and the Embassy in terms of strength of field. You can't discount the overseas players, of course − I was beaten in the first round by New Zealand's Ivan Botica in 1989 and by Australia's Ian Schuback in the second round in 1990 − but the extra UK presence in the CIS gives the field greater depth, because all the players specialize in indoor bowls.

Playing on the portable rink itself is unlike playing anywhere else. The rink, made up of wooden pallets, levelled by lasers, is well nigh perfect − but it does change a lot with temperature as the TV lights bake it. Then, of course, playing bowls with the spectators so close on both sides of the rink takes some getting used to.

I love it. To me it's bowls at its best − although, at the same time, I must say that I enjoy playing outdoors with the sun on my back. But, for presentation, and theatre, you couldn't wish for a better advertisement for our game. The professionalism of the WIBC; their insight in appointing David Harrison to the post of Tournament Director; and the boost of having bowls televised by the BBC: all these things have enhanced the image of bowls.

I even enjoy reading the changes on the rink —
though sometimes they have caught me out!
Although I have won my fair share on the portable
rink, I have yet to win the world indoor singles on
it. I have wonderful memories of my three wins at
Coatbridge — and I am looking forward to winning
the world indoor title sometime on the portable
rink.

I regard my victory over Bob Sutherland, then
world champion, in the 1983 UK final as one of the
best performances of my career, but I was delighted
to win the same championship again in 1989, when
I escaped from almost certain defeat against David
Corkill. And my two wins in the Superbowl suggest
that the portable rink, designed by a friend of mine,
Mike Williams from Bristol, has been a happy
hunting ground.

DRJ

Most of my commentating is done these days at
Preston, where the portable rink fits snugly into the
grand hall. Bowls is so suited to television, and the
studio atmosphere created by building a set around
the rink makes for pure theatre. I thought the same
when I visited the Crucible a few years ago to watch
the Embassy world snooker. The lights, hush, incredible skill and quiet conflict between one player
and another equal absolute magic. A thrilling *pièce
de théâtre.*

And there is no bowler more suited to the role of
leading man than DJB. His stage presence is alarm-
ing. He is so relaxed and clearly at home centre
stage. All the other performers are spear-carriers by
comparison. And, judging by the grannies — and
stage-struck *ingénues* — queuing up for his auto-
graph after a match, he's the ultimate matinée idol.

Even the games he loses have a five-star rating in
my book. Like the time — in 1986 — he came back
from a 4-sets-to-nil deficit to tie with Steve Rees at
4-sets-all in the UK final. There is a special brand of
Bryant magic, maybe something to do with that
pipe — the thing that is his most popular trademark

(yet something which does attract criticism from the no-smoking brigade).

One thing is certain. Since television took an interest in bowls, the general public have sat up and taken notice. The qualities of our game have received a wider audience, and the main characters in the drama have become household names. Bowls, whether you watch it live from the front row in the Preston Guild Hall, or at home on the box from the comfort of your favourite armchair, has become a popular spectator sport.

10 SOME GOOD EXAMPLES

Great players can serve as good examples to those who aspire to follow in their footsteps. The authors, between them, have more than eighty years' experience in the game, and have met and been influenced by some of the greatest players in the world.

There is much more to learn than technique. More than tactics, too. Exemplary green behaviour, and a high standard of sportsmanship are hallmarks of the really great player. It is surprising, in fact, that there are so few players of world class who let the side down in this respect.

TONY ALLCOCK MBE (Cheltenham and England)

Tony Allcock is probably the most successful bowler in the world today — certainly in the increasingly important world of indoor bowls. He has won the Embassy world indoor singles title twice, and the world indoor pairs four times.

Outdoors, too, he has had outstanding success at world level, winning the triples gold in 1980, fours gold and pairs silver in 1984, fours bronze and pairs silver in 1988. Since the introduction of a ranking system, grading indoor singles players, he has consistently come out as Britain's number one.

DJB

I have partnered Tony to many of his successes, starting with the world triples in 1980, and I can confirm that he is the complete all-round player with two or four bowls.

Not only is he master of the singles game — as seen on TV — but he is equally effective as a skip, as

I can testify after leading for him in seven world pairs championships. He inspires his partners, and brings out the best in them.

His own strengths are his immaculate drawing shots, but, more especially, his ability to 'read' the green, and quickly produce a range of outstanding running shots, with varying degrees of weight and arc. He is an unorthodox player, but supremely and naturally talented.

NORMA SHAW MBE (Ropner Park, County Durham and England)

Norma Shaw is commonly regarded as the best woman bowler in the world, although Mavis Steele, also of England, and, more recently, Ireland's Margaret Johnston have also laid claim to that title. Certainly, however, Norma was the most successful woman bowler of the 1980s.

Having won the world outdoor title in 1981, she has also collected a record number of English and

Norma Shaw with
DJB.
(Ken Beetham)

British titles, both in team events and, more especially, in singles.

DJB

Norma has been the perfect advertisement for women's bowls, and has competed in many televised mixed singles events, beating most of the top men.

She is a beautiful drawing player, who can also attack when necessary, and she possesses a fine temperament, which has enabled her to remain calm through many a crisis, and win games she looked like losing.

MAVIS STEELE, MBE (Egham and England)

Mavis Steele has been the outstanding woman bowler in England (if not the world) over a spell of thirty years. She gained her first international honours for England in 1959, and is still a regular in the national side.

She has won more England titles than anyone else, including the singles three times, and skipped England's four to the world title in Canada in 1981 — winning the silver in the triples the same year.

Not only has she been a tireless and successful

Mavis Steele.
(Duncan Cubitt/ Bowls International Magazine)

player over three decades, she has become one of the stalwart administrators of the women's game. The Assistant Secretary of the English Women's Bowling Association (EWBA), she was President of the English Women's Indoor Bowling Association (EWIBA) for the 1989−90 winter season.

DJB

Mavis has been a contemporary of mine, and I feel proud to have known her. She is one of the few players to have been included in Her Majesty's New Year's Honours List, and was awarded the MBE in 1983.

On the green, her approach is intimidating. A good drawing player, she is also adept with the drive, a weapon relatively sparingly used among women bowlers. Her ability to skip a rink is second to none. Mavis is a real General.

RICHARD CORSIE (Craigentinny and Scotland)

Although he is still a very young player (he won the

Richard Corsie.
*(Duncan Cubitt/
Bowls
International
Magazine)*

world indoor title when he was twenty-two years of age) Richard has been on the scene for some years, having won the Scottish and British junior titles when he was only sixteen.

He represented Scotland in the Commonwealth Games at Edinburgh in 1986, aged nineteen, and won the bronze medal, repeating the achievement in Auckland four years later. He has also won major events in Australia and Hong Kong.

DJB

I have noticed how Richard's game has matured in the last few years, culminating in his marvellous display against Willie Wood in the 1989 world indoor final. I experienced something of his skill at first-hand in Auckland in 1990, when he beat me to the bronze medal.

One of the fastest drivers in the game, he has rationed the use of this weapon in recent years, and has been more successful for that. When he is in form, his delivery action is a fine example of all that is desirable. It possesses rhythm, flow, suppleness and a perfect follow-through.

His whole body moves beautifully down the line, maintaining perfect balance at all times. His style is well worth studying in detail.

HUGH DUFF (Drongan and Scotland)

Hugh Duff was twenty-four years of age when he won the Embassy world indoor singles championship in 1988 with a sublime exhibition of drawing play. His bowls seemed to have a magnetic attraction for the jack.

His success was a reward for a dedicated approach, involving assiduous practice — mainly at his home indoor stadium in Auchinleck, Ayrshire, where he spent his formative bowling years

Hugh Duff.
(Duncan Cubitt/ Bowls International Magazine)

Willie Wood with DJB.

grooving his delivery until it resembled a bowling machine.

DJB

I remember playing Hugh at Auchinleck, and again, not long afterwards, in the semi-final of the world indoor singles at Coatbridge in 1987. I had great trouble beating him — by the odd set in five — and I formed the opinion there and then that he was destined to be a future world champion.

Little did I know then that he would achieve the highest accolade the very next year — with that superb display of drawing at Alexandra Palace. Among his assets are a high level of self-confidence, a calm temperament, and a rare dedication to the game. He tends to specialize in singles play, and has it down to a fine art.

WILLIE WOOD (Gifford and Scotland)

Willie started playing at the age of twelve, taught by

his father, William Edward Wood. He won his first club title in 1952 — when he was fourteen — and has been one of the game's most consistent players.

He has won medals in the five continents of the world — probably the only player to have done so. Willie was the Commonwealth Games singles champion at Brisbane in 1982, and added another gold — the fours — at Auckland in 1990.

DJB

I have known Willie as a friend and rival for many years, and consider him to be a great all-round player. He served his apprenticeship leading for Scotland for several years before being selected to play at the 'back-end'.

Jim Baker
(Duncan Cubitt/ Bowls International Magazine)

He thinks deeply about the game, and is a sound tactician who can play all the shots. He draws the best out of his team-mates − this was proved again at Auckland − and is one of the game's great characters. He is a tremendous singles player, whom I have met on the green many, many times. I am proud to have known him.

JIM BAKER (Cliftonville and Ireland)

Jim Baker was first capped for Ireland in 1979 − at the age of twenty-one − since when he has developed into one of the outstanding all-round players in the world.

He won two world championships − one indoors and one out − in 1984, beating teenager Nigel Smith in the Embassy final, then skipping Stan Espie and Sammy Allen to the world outdoor triples title at Aberdeen.

Adding the world outdoor fours title in 1988, he had to settle for silver in the Commonwealth Games at Auckland in 1990, when his Irish four lost to Willie Wood's Scottish quartet. He won the CIS UK singles in 1985, and became the first Irishman to win the Bushmills Irish Masters at Ballymoney in January 1990.

DJB

Jim is one of Britain's finest skips, having repeatedly proved his ability to play pressure shots at world level. He is a born leader, and knows exactly how to get the best out of his men.

He can play all the shots, but he is perhaps particularly spectacular with his drive, putting all his bodyweight behind the shot, and achieving an impressive strike-rate.

DAVID CORKILL (Knock and Ireland)

David Corkill is one of the game's most exciting and successful players, having won the British singles title indoors and out, the Superbowl (twice) and many other top events all over the world over a period of more than ten years.

David Corkill.
*(Duncan Cubitt/
Bowls
International
Magazine)*

**Margaret
Johnston.**
*(Duncan Cubitt/
Bowls
International
Magazine)*

Nicknamed 'The Pink Panther', he lopes after his bowl with an exaggerated low follow-through, and possesses one of the most distinctive delivery actions in the game.

DJB

David is a colourful player, and a great tactical thinker. He loves to really 'get involved' in the game, and, when he finds his rhythm, he can be a very hard man to beat.

He plays all the shots, and has a more 'professional' attitude than most of the top players. Everyone remembers his exciting last-gasp victory over Margaret Johnston in the 1988 Superbowl final.

MARGARET JOHNSTON (Ballymoney and Ireland)

A beginner could do a lot worse than to study Margaret Johnston's delivery. Not only is she arguably the most successful woman bowler in the world today, but she is one of the best stylists in the game.

She has adapted to the full-length game from short mat bowls, which is very popular in Ireland, and has won the British singles title indoors and out. She has also won the world indoor title, and earned a gold for pairs and silver for singles at the 1988 world outdoor championships.

With Freda Elliott, she won the pairs gold medal at the Commonwealth Games in 1986, and it was a surprise to many that she failed to win the singles in 1990. Papua New Guinea's Geua Tau, however, who beat her in the section at Auckland and went on to win the gold medal, also sets a good example − keeping the game simple, and making no fuss. What a good temperament!

DJB

I have watched Margaret beat a lot of my male colleagues in televised events, and rate her as one of the most consistent players around. I hope I will not be branded 'sexist' if I suggest she plays the game like a man. I hope that will be taken the right way, because I certainly mean it as a compliment.

Let me explain what I mean. Women have not had the opportunity to develop their game in competition with the best of the men – until recently, anyway. And the women's game is still dominated by the draw. Given a choice, it seems to me, most women will opt for the drawing shot as opposed to the drive every time.

There is no reason why women cannot play the heavy shots – even if most are unable to muster the strength of a Belliss, Corsie or Parrella. The best of the women are increasing their repertoire, and are beginning to play a more aggressive game. Margaret can certainly play the attacking shot, as she showed in the Superbowl final in 1988, when David Corkill only just managed to beat her, 7-6, in the deciding set.

ROB PARRELLA (Australia)

Rob Parrella was born in Italy, and brings a Mediterranean flavour to his play. He is Australia's most successful singles player in recent years, although he was surprisingly ignored by the selectors after he won the silver medal behind Willie Wood in 1982.

A controversial figure who likes to make his presence felt on the green, Rob inspires a reaction in spectators, who are equally divided between those who love him and those who loathe him. There is no denying that he is one of the most exciting players, and a great entertainer.

DJB

Rob's crowning achievement was winning the gold medal in the Commonwealth Games at Auckland in 1990. He beat me to the gold medal play-off, using his drive to good effect. I can confirm that he is the most accurate driver in the game – and one of the fastest, too.

His success with the drive is due to his perfect natural balance, and he is particularly deadly on the ultra-fast greens of the southern hemisphere. He is

Rob Parrella.
*(Duncan Cubitt/
Bowls
International
Magazine)*

also one of the few players down under who favour the cradle grip.

IAN SCHUBACK (Hills District and Australia)

Ian Schuback took up bowls in 1982 after watching England's Mal Hughes on television during the 1980 world championships at Frankston — and only four years later he was in Edinburgh, winning the silver medal in the Commonwealth Games.

Inexplicably, he was left out of the Australian team to play in the sixth World Bowls in 1988, but was back in action at Auckland for the 1990 Commonwealth Games, when he won the pairs gold medal as lead to Trevor Morris.

He made a great impact on bowls in Britain when, with Jim Yates, he won the world indoor

Ian Schuback.
*(Duncan Cubitt/
Bowls
International
Magazine)*

pairs title at the Bournemouth International Centre in 1987, and reached two finals at the Embassy championships in 1990.

DJB

Ian's approach to the game offers a good model to the ambitious beginner. He is dedicated, disciplined and professional, practises hard, and is meticulous in his approach to delivery and shot selection.

He also clearly believes that the more you put into life the more you get out of it, for he spends a great deal of time and energy preparing for his matches, and goes into each match brimful of confidence.

JOHN SNELL (Australia)

John Snell won singles silver medals at Commonwealth and world level, and has amassed a great number of State and Invitation Masters titles in his

native Australia.

Something of a specialist in singles play, he is one of the great thinkers of the game, and one of the most respected players in his home country.

DJB

It always impressed me that John had developed his own firing technique, imparting a 'flicker' to his bowl on delivery so that it kept on line for longer before the bias started to take effect.

It is not, in my opinion, a trick to be recommended, but it certainly worked for him, and was the result of scientific theory being applied to technique. The idea appealed to me, however, because I, too, have developed my own 'tricks of the trade' from my own theories.

These personal features of delivery might not suit everyone, but the principle of working out ideas for yourself, and developing your own personal delivery is to be recommended.

I had — and have — a great respect for John, who, in my opinion, is one of the greatest ambassadors for bowls Australia has ever produced.

PETER BELLISS MBE (Aramoho and New Zealand)

Peter Belliss, though he is known for his ferocious drive that strikes fear into the hearts of opponents and spectators alike, is also one of the most delicate drawing players in the world.

He visited Britain several times in the early Eighties to play in the Jack High Masters at Worthing, and studied the British game so professionally that he was able to win the world singles title at Aberdeen in 1984.

His solid stance, and rhythmic delivery are well worth studying, and a beginner could do worse

Peter Belliss.
(Duncan Cubitt/ Bowls International Magazine)

than take him as a model when searching for a good style to emulate.

DJB

Peter impressed me in the early days when he first came to England. A lot of players from the southern hemisphere give up when they encounter our greens – which are much heavier than the ones they are used to.

He got to grips with the problem, soon realizing that his favourite weapon – the drive – was never going to be as effective in the UK as it was back home. His maturity in adjusting to the new conditions was exemplary, and definitely something from which everyone can learn a lesson.

PHIL SKOGLUND (Palmerston North and New Zealand)

According to most New Zealanders, Phil Skoglund is that country's greatest-ever bowler. Phil started young, winning the New Zealand singles in 1958, when he was only twenty-one, since when he has collected just about every title available in his home country.

His record away from home has not been so impressive, although he did collect the silver medal for skipping New Zealand's four into the world final at Aberdeen in 1984, and another for reaching the world indoor singles final in 1986.

After representing his country in world championships and Commonwealth Games since 1966, his gold medal performance in the world triples championship at Auckland in 1988 was one of the most popular wins of all time.

He has a most unusual delivery – especially for a fast green player. His backswing is enormous, and involves raising the bowl almost to head level before commencing the forward swing. As the forward swing continues, however, Phil slows the action down, so that the bowl is delivered with great control and finesse.

DJB

I have known Phil for many, many years, and have a lot of respect for him — both as a bowler and a man. Like all Kiwis, he is a very accurate driver, but make no mistake, he can draw beautifully as well — particularly on the fast New Zealand greens.

He is another one of those great skips who demand respect from their players, and earn it both with their play and their behaviour on the green.

Phil Skoglund.
(Duncan Cubitt/ Bowls International Magazine)

11 BOWLING ABROAD

Although bowls was 'born' in Britain, it is now a popular game the world over, especially in Commonwealth countries. The International Bowling Board (IBB) comprises thirty countries, with ten full members, fifteen associate members, and five affiliate members.

British-born, bowls is now popular worldwide

We like to think that the United Kingdom is the hotbed of bowls, and British teams certainly tend to dominate world events. There will be many in the southern hemisphere, however, who would contest our view that Britain is best, because bowls is booming in Australia and New Zealand.

AUSTRALIA

In Australia, bowls, despite the claims of cricket, Rugby Union, Rugby League and Australian Rules Football, could be described as the national sport. More people play bowls than any other sport, and there are more bowlers per head of the Australian population than anywhere else in the world.

Curiously, the average age of bowlers in Australia is still pretty high. The game has not yet recruited young men on the scale we have experienced in Britain. True there are those like Trevor Morris and Ian Schuback, Dennis Katunarich and Paul Richards who have made a name for themselves before they have turned forty — but they are the exceptions rather than the rule.

Nevertheless, the game is very well established, and tremendously well organized. The quality of the greens, the affluence of the clubs, the acceptance of coaching methods and the intensity of competi-

DJB rates the Australian greens as the best in the world.

tion puts bowls in Australia into a different league from the charming, amateur game it is in England.

In Britain, we have seen the burgeoning of the indoor game in recent years, when its success has been guaranteed by commercial pressures. Unlike the outdoor game, indoor bowls has become big business in Britain: it was always so, outdoors, in Australia.

In Australian cities, clubs with just one six-rink green simply do not exist. It is usual for a club to have three, four, or even five greens — serving maybe 500 or so members. Palatial clubhouses are run on business lines, and the greens are tended, not by a club member in his spare time, but by a head greenkeeper who controls a staff of four or five or more.

While the scale of the clubs, and the elegance of

the clubhouses are the first things that surprise visitors from the UK, the standard of the playing surfaces presents the biggest contrast of all. Australian greens, by and large, are superb.

Firstly, they are much faster than British greens. A bowl delivered with only enough pace to reach a short jack on the average British green would rocket into the ditch in Australia. While Brits think of a 13 second green as being pretty free, few Australian greens would run as slow.

Remember, to 'time' a green you count the seconds it takes for a bowl to come to rest 30 yards (27.4m) away from the delivery mat. The longer it takes to stop, the faster the green. On a slow green, it is necessary to hurl the bowl at great speed, and the long, wet grass stops it in its tracks in no time at all – so, curiously, the 'slow' green produces a 'fast' time.

In Britain, our start-of-season greens often run at around 9 or 10 seconds, and can be expected to pick up speed mid-summer to around 12 or 13 seconds. Occasionally, in a particularly dry spell, we might get a green running as quickly as 14 seconds.

Australia is a big place, so speeds will differ from north to south, as the greens respond to climatic influences. In the south, where it is cooler, greens may run at around 13 or 14 seconds; in New South Wales, at 15 to 16 seconds; in Queensland, up to 17 and 18 seconds, and even faster on occasions.

The difference between British and Australian greens is only partly a matter of climate. Just as important is the priority the Australians give to producing greens of a high standard – and the time, effort, expertise and money they lavish on their playing surfaces. Australian greens are cut and rolled every day.

British greens are very green, with a succulent growth of shallow-rooting grass; they are soft and they allow the bowl to 'bed in' or 'track' as it travels down the rink. Australian greens are yellow/brown in colour; they are dry and covered with very deep-rooting grass; watered sparingly, they are often bone-hard, and they do not allow the bowl to sink in at all.

Our fine, shallow-rooting grasses would not survive in Australian temperatures. They play on couch grass or bent — or a type of grass known as tift-dwarf. Couch is more suited to the very hot temperatures in Queensland, around Cairns, because it is resilient, while bent grass is more popular in the southern states.

Some of the New South Wales and Queensland clubs are able to stay open for twelve months in the year, with many of the southern bowlers moving north to play in tournaments in the winter months.

Most competitive play goes on at weekends, because of the comparatively short evenings — though some clubs are now equipped with floodlights to give extra hours during the week. League play between the clubs is the staple diet in Australia, with every club putting out more than one team in an attempt to win a pennant.

The winner of the season's league is proud to fly the pennant the following year. Invitation Masters events are also popular, as are open tournaments, including the national championships, played in each state in turn, without the prolonged qualification process employed in Britain.

The same principle applies in New Zealand and the USA, where the nationals are a holiday event, similar to seaside tournaments in the UK. If you want to enter, you can, but if the venue is not in your own state, you may have to travel across the continent to do so.

Each year there are, of course, more entries from the local state than from those further afield. Some intrepid bowlers appear in the nationals every year, but many top bowlers feel unable to enter because they can afford neither the time nor the cost of travel and accommodation.

DJB

I first visited Australia in 1962, when I played for England in the Commonwealth Games in Perth.

The Dalkeith greens were a joy to play on, cut and rolled every day, and perfectly level, but the first thing that struck me was the high level of organization, and the intensity of competition, especially at the top level.

I soon realized that the standard of the greens and the importance given to coaching were major factors in Australian success at bowls. The emphasis on producing level, fast-running greens has given players the opportunity to develop their skills in a much more controlled way than is possible in Britain.

With our greens, we may be more adaptable − we have to be! − but Aussie greens, like billiard tables, put a premium on control and pure skill. Concentration is vital, fine control essential − but you get what you deserve.

I love Australian greens. British bowls can sometimes be a lottery − especially outdoors. But down under you miss your line at your peril, and a bowl delivered with too much weight is always punished. You really have to hold the bowl back, and, above all, give it the green!

Hurling the bowl up the green − as we have to do so often in Britain simply to reach the jack − is never necessary. Putting bodyweight into your delivery is disastrous. You must try to keep your bodyweight back, and that is done, quite simply, by dropping your right knee as you deliver.

Launching your bowl so that it goes well into the next rink takes some getting used to − but is often necessary on greens faster than 15 seconds. You have to believe it will come back − and it will! On such greens, it is always better to over-estimate the angle required, because the bias will almost certainly bring the bowl back more than you imagined, while a narrow bowl will swing uselessly out of the picture.

Since my first visit in 1962, I have always had a soft spot for Australia, and have returned time and time again. Sydney beckoned in 1966, Melbourne in 1980, but, in between, I visited Newcastle, Banyon,

Adelaide, Waratah, and many other places, for Masters events of all kinds.

I remember with affection all my opponents in the big events: Dr Leigh Fitzpatrick in 1962; Geoff Kelly, who won the pairs with Bert Palm in 1966; John Snell, who won the silver medal in 1980. I met Glyn Bosisto in 1966, and really enjoyed the company of my fellow-competitors in the Banyo Masters in 1971.

Frank Soars, Barry Salter, Errol Bungay, Stewie Shannon, Keith Dwyer, Merv Davey, Artie Booth and John Snell were a marvellous bunch, and typified the hospitality I have always received whenever I have been lucky enough to visit Australia.

NEW ZEALAND

Greens in New Zealand are even faster than those in Australia, but arguments rage over the relative merits of those in the South Island as opposed to the North — and of the cotula greens as opposed to the grass greens.

Cotula — a swamp weed — is now the most common covering for greens in New Zealand, and is a beautiful surface to play on. The weed once was regarded as a menace, until greenkeepers had the bright notion of giving the weed its head, and letting it take over.

It has broad leaves, which curl up in the heat of the sun, and flatten out, like miniature water-lilies in the wet. This means that the greens actually speed up in the rain — until the green becomes waterlogged, like it did at Henderson during the 1988 world championships and at Pakuranga during the 1990 Commonwealth Games.

DJB

Bowls in New Zealand is a draw-drive game. Greens are so fast that it is virtually impossible to play the controlled weight shot with any degree of success. Drawing to the jack needs a delicate touch, and firing is the favourite alternative.

New Zealanders are probably the best drivers in

the world. With practice, and a good eye, it is possible to become very accurate with the drive or firing shot – as experts like Peter Belliss and Phil Skoglund have demonstrated.

I love fast greens, but it always takes time to get used to the speed of greens down under. We are used to bowling within a range of speeds from 9 to 14 seconds in the UK, and the average surface in New Zealand is outside that range altogether.

On my last two visits, I have experimented with a new delivery, and have found it a successful way of coping with the quickest of greens. Keeping my basic crouch stance, I have grounded the bowl prior to delivery rather than cup it, caress it and 'jiggle' it to develop a rhythm.

Starting with the bowl at ground level, it is impossible to relax into a long backswing, and much easier to keep your bodyweight back. Movement is kept to a minimum, and impetus is imparted with wrist and fingers.

When British players return home after a few weeks in New Zealand, they invariably struggle to reach the jack. My first attempts always finish embarrassingly halfway up the rink! No wonder the Kiwis and Aussies – who have never experienced heavy greens – are baffled and bewildered when they come to our shores.

Some of my happiest times have been spent in New Zealand. It was in Christchurch that I won one of my Commonwealth Games gold medals in 1974, and in Auckland that I won my third world singles title in 1988. Losing to Rob Parrella in the Commonwealth Games in 1990 was disappointing, of course, but, again, it was a great event.

One of my favourite off-the-green memories is of a great sea fishing trip with Remuera's Jack Bennett in 1988. Like the Australians, the New Zealanders may have a tradition of pommie-bashing, but I must say I have been accorded the most generous hospitality, and have always found Aussies and Kiwis the very best of company.

HONG KONG

For such a small bowling country, Hong Kong has produced some of the most competitive and successful players in the world. With fewer than 1,000 bowlers, Hong Kong won two out of three gold medals in the Commonwealth Games at Edmonton in 1978, and seem to be in line for more success in future from the excitingly talented Mark McMahon.

Greens in Hong Kong are not of the highest standard, but this does not deter their players in any way. Indeed, all the colony's stars seem to pick out a very good line — perhaps because lines are hard to find at home.

DJB

Bowls seems to attract all-round sportsmen and women in Hong Kong. George Souza, who beat me in the final of the Gateway Masters, was a hockey international, and so was M. B. Hassan, who lived for a while in England, and played alongside DRJ and myself at Clevedon.

George's father was a good player, too, and I always had a lot of respect for Eric Liddell. Philip Chok reached the final of the world indoor singles championship in 1980, O. K. Dallah was a regular visitor to Worthing, and now the McMahon family have created a unique record, with Mark's mum (Rosemary) and dad (Bill) lining up alongside him in the colony's Commonwealth Games side.

One thing is certain, whenever you are drawn against Hong Kong, you can be sure you are in for a tough game.

SOUTH AFRICA

South Africa were – and probably still are – one of the great bowling nations. They proved it in 1976, when they won all four events in the world championships in Johannesburg, since when, for political reasons, they have not been able to test their strength against the rest of the world.

Greens are reputedly very good, and the competition intense. The climate, certainly, helps. Doug

Watson won the singles in 1976, and Bill Moseley won the Jack High Masters at Worthing twice in succession before the Gleneagles agreement curtailed his participation.

CANADA AND THE USA

Although there are plenty of clubs in both North American countries, the big distances between them make selection very difficult. Bowls is played in Florida, Los Angeles, New York and Chicago on a wide variety of surfaces, none of them particularly good.

In Canada, frost plays havoc with the greens, although, by all accounts, there are some good greens in Vancouver. Short summers do not help, and it is really quite surprising that indoor bowls has been slow to take off.

Bowlers like Ron Jones and Bill Boettger have become quite well known in Britain, and Burnie Gill forced his way into the Embassy world indoor singles final in 1983. The USA, however, has a better record in world events, having won the triples in 1972 and the pairs in 1984.

Perhaps it should be mentioned that Skippy Arculli's success in the pairs was achieved in partnership with a Scot, George Adrain, who came in as a locally provided reserve for Jimmy Candelet, who hurt his leg, and could not play after the first game.

THE EMERGING COUNTRIES

Papua New Guinea's success in the Commonwealth Games in 1990, when Geua Tau won the women's singles gold medal, was a major fillip for the game in the south sea islands.

Several leading Australians visit PNG regularly, and their coaching and encouragement are certainly paying off. The Fijians are also capable of springing surprises, and it is good to see Norfolk Island, the Cook Islands, Singapore, India, and Japan beginning to enter the major world championships.

The African countries — Kenya, Swaziland, Zimbabwe, Botswana, Malawi and Zambia — do not

boast a great membership, but are regular competi-
tors, while Argentina has caused an upset or two.
Jose Riveros beat Willie Wood in 1988, and the
Argentinian four beat Australia in 1984.

Closer to home, the Channel Islands produce
keen players, and the bowlers in Guernsey now
have the advantage of a handsome new indoor
stadium to give them continuity, and it appears as if
bowls may be set to go into Europe. There are
already several clubs in Spain, and television coverage has introduced the indoor game to Holland and
Belgium.

12 BOWLS ORGANIZATIONS AND ADDRESSES

WHO'S WHO AND WHAT'S WHAT?

This chapter is intended to help experienced bowlers as well as beginners to find their way around the game. There are so many organizations looking after the game — indoors and out — for men and for women — flat green and crown — association and federation — clubs, counties, and national associations. No wonder people get confused!

The game is very, very old — and exceedingly simple. Rolling a ball at a given target is a natural thing to do. Skittles; ten-, nine-, seven- and five-pin bowling; *bocca; petanque; boules;* and even marbles: all these derive from the same origins.

Bowls, with biased woods, was first played anywhere a relatively flat piece of ground could be found. I don't imagine they played on rinks on Plymouth Hoe, when Sir Francis Drake kept everyone, including the Spaniards, waiting while he attempted to draw the winner.

When rinks were thought of, and greens were specially constructed to be as level as possible, there were others who preferred to go on playing on undulating ground — the ups and downs gave the game its special challenge. That's the difference between crown green and flat green bowls.

CROWN GREEN

Crown green, played under the rules of the British Crown Green Bowling Association (BCGBA), is exceedingly popular in England's northern counties — but is virtually unknown anywhere else in the world. The greens are constructed with a raised centre − rather like an up-turned saucer − with play permissible in any direction.

The bowls themselves are slightly smaller than flat green woods, and are less heavily biased. Two-wood play is standard, and the usual format is singles, sometimes pairs − never triples or fours. The jack itself is biased, and is larger than the flat green jack.

Greens are often adjacent to pubs or working men's clubs, or situated in the local park. There are few private clubs. Money prizes have long been part of the crown green scene, and a 'panel' of crown green professionals pointed the way for the recent flat green excursion into the world of big business.

FEDERATION BOWLS

Like the crown green variety, Federation bowls is restricted to one region of England. It is played in thirteen eastern counties from Northumberland to Essex, and extends inland as far as Nottingham and Derby and Wisbech.

Although the English Bowling Federation (EBF) decrees that the game should be played on rinks, there are clubs who still play the roving jack form of bowls, where the jack is not centred before play begins.

Jack and bowls are identical to those used in the mainstream flat green game, and some clubs actually play both codes on the same green, but there are several interesting variations in the Laws of the Game.

The EBF does not recognize − or reward − touchers. Thus, woods that find their way into the ditch are dead, even if they touched the jack. No bowl that is more than 6 feet (1.83m) from the jack can count as a shot. Fours is not played at all, and the EBF in fact use the word, 'rinks', for their standard game of two-wood triples.

OUTDOOR AND INDOOR

Outdoors, the game worldwide is administered by

the International Bowling Board (IBB), which at present has thirty countries in membership. Each country has a national association, and, in the case of England, there is a tight structure of county associations which exercise some form of democratic control. The four home countries form the British Isles Bowling Council (BIBC).

Although the indoor game was born in Britain, and has yet to develop throughout the world, the international body is the World Indoor Bowls Council (WIBC). Australia and New Zealand are prominent members, even though indoor greens are few and far between down under, while Guernsey, with one impressive stadium, provided the WIBC President, Henry Le Tissier, in 1990.

In England, there are nearly 300 indoor stadiums, each of which has a vote at the English Indoor Bowling Association's (EIBA) AGM. England, of course, joins with Ireland, Scotland and Wales to form the British Isles Indoor Bowls Council (BIIBC). Counties, although they exist, do not have the same part to play in the running of the EIBA as they do outdoors.

MEN AND WOMEN

Although the top women who have been invited to play in various televised events have proved beyond doubt that women are every bit as good as men when it comes to playing bowls, the administration of the game for men and women is entirely separate.

For every association — club, county, national, British, and world — run by and for the men, there seems to be an equivalent organization for women. Whether this separatism will survive is an interesting question. It would surely be to everyone's advantage if the administration of the game were to be carried out at least from the same office.

Indoor and outdoor associations, as well as men and women, could surely be more efficiently run if they shared the same printing, computer and secretarial facilities. And people interested in the game

– like potential sponsors, television producers, the Sports Council, as well as beginners – would know where to go with any queries about the game.

COACHING

Each of the four home countries is committed to the value of coaching, and has appointed a national coach. In England, the English Bowls Coaching Scheme (EBCS) shows the way to the national associations themselves by coaching across the board, with no distinction made between the sexes, codes or associations.

Thus, the EBCS serves men and women bowlers indoors and out – whether they play crown or flat green or the Federation game. Harry De'ath, the EBCS Chairman, is particularly proud of this umbrella function, and the Sports Council is also delighted with the arrangement.

PLAYERS ASSOCIATIONS

The input of top players into the administration and development of the game is an important factor – but decision-making was for too long in the hands of amateur administrators, some of whom were out of touch with the game – particularly at top level. Little consultation ever actually happened.

In 1980, the English Bowls Players Association (EBPA) was formed, and the Scottish Indoor Bowls Players Association (SIBPA) followed a few years later. Players have found a voice, and the views of the top exponents of the game may now be expressed. Players involved in the hurly-burly of competition may have little time to devote as administrators, but wise administrators will listen to what they have to say.

The roles of both the English and Scottish Players Associations will expand in future, and surely the other countries will follow suit. Perhaps the time is approaching when a British Players Association may be formed – or a world body that could represent the views of players during events like the world championships – indoors and out.

ADDRESSES

UNITED KINGDOM

British Isles Bowling Council
Secretary: A. Richmond McKay
43 Belfast Road
Ballynure
Ballyclare
Co. Antrim BT39 9TZ **(09603) 52334**

British Isles Women's Bowling Council
Secretary: Nancie Colling
Darracombe
The Clays
Market Lavington
Wiltshire SN10 4AY **(0380) 813774**

British Isles Indoor Bowls Council
Secretary: Martin Conlin
8/2 Backdean
Ravelston Terrace
Edinburgh EH4 3EF **(031) 343 3632**

British Isles Women's Indoor Bowls Council
Secretary: Joan Johns
16 Windsor Crescent
Radyr
Cardiff CF4 8AE **(0222) 842391**

British Crown Green Bowling Association
Secretary: Ron Holt
14 Leighton Avenue
Maghull
Liverpool L31 0AH **(051) 526 8367**

ENGLAND

English Bowls Council
Secretary: Eric Crosbie
15 Datchworth Court
Village Road
Enfield
Middlesex EN1 2DS **(081) 367 1269**

English Bowling Association
Secretary: David W. Johnson
Lyndhurst Road
Worthing
West Sussex BN11 2AZ **(0903) 820222**

English Women's Bowling Association
Secretary: Nancie Colling
Darracombe
The Clays
Market Lavington
Wiltshire SN10 4AY **(0380) 813774**

English Bowling Federation
Secretary: John Webb
62 Frampton Place
Boston
Lincs PE21 8EL **(0205) 366201**

English Women's Bowling Federation
Secretary: Ivy Younger
Irela
Holburn Crescent
Ryton
Tyne and Wear NE40 3DH **(091) 413 3160**

English Indoor Bowling Association
Secretary: Bernard Telfer
290A Barking Road
London E6 3BA **(081) 470 1237**

English Women's Indoor Bowling Association
Secretary: Pam Allison
Jadrah
8 Oakfield Road
Carterton
Oxford OX8 3RB **(0993) 841344**

English Bowls Players Association
President: David J. Bryant CBE
Secretary: David Crocker
5 The Ridgeway
Edenbridge
Kent TN8 6AU **(0732) 863894**

English Bowls Umpires' Association
Secretary: Norman S. Deeprose
24 Elm Green Close
Worcester WR5 3HD **(0905) 350717**
Area Secretaries:
Northern: N. D. Williams
3 Trent Avenue
Thornaby on Tees
Cleveland TS17 8HS **(0642) 672054**
Midlands: J. E. Brooks
21 Valley Prospect
Newark
Notts NG24 4QH **(0636) 702730**
Eastern: G. Henderson
50 Manser Road
Rainham
Essex RM13 8NL **(04027) 55613**
S. Eastern: B. Ticehurst
6 Shakespeare House
3 Shakespeare Road
Worthing
West Sussex BN11 4AN **(0903) 202162**
S. Central: R. F. Henery
117 Marlborough Road
Swindon
Wilts SN3 1NJ **(0793) 538666**

S. Western: A. R. Quick
10 Wearde Road
Saltash
Cornwall PL12 4NP **(0752) 842420**

English Bowls Umpires' Federation (EBF)
Secretary: Cecil A. Kemp
5 Milton Street
Ipswich
Suffolk IP4 4PP **(0473) 725259**

English Bowls Coaching Scheme
Chairman: Harry A. C. De'ath
40 Clive Avenue
Ipswich
Suffolk IP1 4LU **(0473) 257407**
National Director of Coaching: Gwyn John
34 Ocean View Road
Bude
Cornwall EX23 8NN **(0288) 352391**

National Coaches for the Regions
Northern: Derek Bell
101 Station Road
Seaton Carew
Hartlepool
Cleveland TS25 1DX **(0429) 67104**
Midland: Vic Cooper
534 Kettering Road North
Northampton NN3 1HN **(0604) 493193**
Central: Tony Hodgkinson
4 Pensfield Park
Charlton Mead Est
Westbury
Bristol BS10 6LD **(0272) 503261**
Eastern: Arthur Meeson
22 Pleasant Rise
Hatfield
Herts AL8 5DU **(07072) 68081**

Southern: Peter A. Line
Flat 2 Elm Court
53 Westwood Road
Southampton SO2 1DX **(0703) 553995**
S. Western: Gwyn John
34 Ocean View Road
Bude
Cornwall EX23 8NN **(0288) 352391**
Crown Green: Graham Preston
27 Maple Close
Chasetown
Walsall
Staffs WS7 8RP **(05436) 71529**
Video Operative: Kelvin Carr
37 Bramley Rise
Strood
Kent ME2 3SU **(0634) 718488**
Video Producer: David Rhys Jones
9 Victoria Road
Clevedon
Avon BS21 7RY **(0272) 877280**

IRELAND

Irish Bowling Association
Secretary: Jim Barnes
212 Sicily Park
Belfast BT10 0AQ **(0232) 614658**

Irish Women's Bowling Association
Secretary: Doreen Sutton
Flat 2 Downview Court
Downview Park West
Belfast BT15 5HZ **(0232) 771427**

Association of Irish Indoor Bowls
Secretary: Billy Burrows
Flat 4 Glenburn Court
Dunmurray
Northern Ireland **(0232) 601025**

Irish Women's Indoor Bowling Association
Secretary: Hazel Getty
25 Knutsford Drive
Belfast BT14 6LZ **(0232) 741678**

SCOTLAND

Scottish Bowling Association
Secretary: Peter Smith
50 Wellington Street
Glasgow G2 6EF **(041) 221 8999**

Scottish Women's Bowling Association
Secretary: Eleanor Allan
5A Esplanade
Greenock PA16 7SD **(0475) 24140**

Scottish Indoor Bowling Association
Secretary: James Barclay
41 Montfode Court
Ardrossan
Ayrshire KA22 7NJ **(0294) 68372**

Scottish Women's Indoor Bowling Association
Secretary: Rita Thompson
1 Underwood Road
Burnside
Rutherglen
Glasgow G73 3TE **(041) 647 5810**

Scottish Indoor Bowls Players Association
President: Bob Sutherland
Secretary: David McGill
61 Ladysmith Road
Edinburgh EH9 1AF **(031) 663 6418**

WALES

Welsh Bowling Association
Secretary: Alan H. Williams
48 Pochin Crescent
Tredegar
Gwent NP2 4JS **(049 525) 3836**

Welsh Women's Bowling Association
Secretary: Linda Parker
Ffrydd Cottages
2 Ffrydd Road
Knighton
Powys LD7 1DB **(0547) 528331**

Welsh Indoor Bowling Association
Secretary: J. Ray Hill
1 Brynheulog Street
Port Talbot
West Glamorgan SA13 1AF **(0639) 886409**

Welsh Women's Indoor Bowling Association
Secretary: Hilary King
Hillcrest Villa
Tynewydd
Treorchy
Rhondda
Mid Glamorgan CF42 5LU **(0443) 771618**

INTERNATIONAL

International Bowling Board
1990-92 President: Jim Barnes (Ireland)
1992-94 President: Alan H. Williams (Wales)
Secretary: David W. Johnson
Lyndhurst Road
Worthing
West Sussex BN11 2AZ **(0903) 820222**

International Women's Bowling Board
President: Pat Weaver (New Zealand)
Secretary: Gloria Oliver
78 Riverbend Road
Napier
New Zealand **(070) 436 819**

World Indoor Bowls Council
Secretary: Jimmy Davidson
44 Stamford Road
Southbourne
Bournemouth BH6 5DS **(0202) 429755**
Tournament Director: David Harrison
PO Box 2
Bakewell
Derby DE4 1TQ **(0629) 87634**

World Indoor Bowls Council (Ladies' Section)
Secretary: Joan Johns
16 Windsor Crescent
Radyr
Cardiff CF4 8AE **(0222) 842391**

Guernsey Bowling Association
Secretary: Simon Masterton
Meadow View
Mount Row
St Peter Port
Guernsey **(0481) 25556**

Jersey Bowling Association
Secretary: Terry Spencer
38 Clubley Estate
New St John's Road
St Helier
Jersey **(0534) 37070**

American Lawn Bowling Association
Secretary: Earl Torango
11660 SW King George
King City
Oregon 97224
USA

Australian Bowls Council
Executive Officer: Al Mewett
Box Q293
Queen Victoria PO
Sydney
NSW 2000
Australia

Canadian Lawn Bowling Council
Executive Director: Margot Clayton Jones
1600 James Naismith Drive
Gloucester
Ontario K1B 5N4
Canada

New Zealand Bowling Association
Secretary: Gordon Mackay
PO Box 65-172
Mairangi Bay
Auckland 10
New Zealand

South African Bowling Association
Secretary: R. B. Heath
15 Keyes Court
Keyes Avenue
Rosebank
Johannesburg 2196
South Africa

Zimbabwe Bowling Association
Secretary: Ivan Waldmeyer
PO Box 1336
Bulawayo
Zimbabwe